A Guide and a History

Cama Beach

Statements and opinions expressed in this book are the author's unless clearly indicated otherwise. The book was financed, written, and published completely independent of the Washington State Parks and Recreation Commission. Quotes and paraphrases of statements by that agency's employees are from the author's notes and interpretations of interviews unless otherwise specified.

Cama Beach: A Guide and a History

Cover, maps, illustrations, and book design by Gary Worthington. Photos not otherwise credited are by the author.

Published by TimeBridges Publishers LLC
4242 Sunset Beach Drive NW
Olympia, WA 98502

On the World Wide Web:
http://www.TimeBridgesPublishers.com

ISBN 978-0-9707662-4-3

Library of Congress Control Number 2008903616

First Edition

Printed and bound in the United States of America
by Gorham Printing, Centralia, WA.

Printed with soy ink on recycled paper.

10 9 8 7 6 5 4 3 2 1

A Guide and a History

Cama Beach

*How a Unique State Park was Created
from a Family Fishing Resort
and a Native American Camping Site*

Gary Worthington

TimeBridges
Publishers
www.TimeBridgesPublishers.com

Also by Gary Worthington:

*India Treasures: An Epic Novel of Rajasthan and Northern India
     through the Ages* (TimeBridges 2001).
     Also published in South Asia as *The Mangarh Chronicles* (Penguin
     India 2002)
*India Fortunes: A Novel of Rajasthan and Northern India through Past
     Centuries* (TimeBridges 2003)

Dedication

To the spirits of the Native American ancestors who used this site over so many centuries.

And to everyone who helped make this magnificent state park possible through vision and dedicated persistence, and by gifts of time, talents, labor, land, and funds.

For Cama Beach State Park to be all that it can be, and for it to nourish the souls of the widest possible range of visitors into the far future, it will continue to need your enthusiastic and generous support.

The Native American Lushootseed language names
for the Cama Beach site include:

Ya-Lked

and

WHEE-uh-PUHK-wuhb
(Place with a small promontory)

Contents

Preface

Often those who use and enjoy a public facility are not aware of how much dedication, work and other resources have gone into providing that experience. Even a book this long cannot adequately convey the extraordinary effort and persistence that went into the creation of Cama Beach State Park, but I try to provide at least some impression of what was involved in that lengthy project.

I wrote this book to fill three needs: (1) A brief guide to the park and its amenities; (2) a history of the site, from its use by Native Americans through its operation as a family resort; and (3) an account of the long, complex, and challenging process of turning the property into a major new state park.

I hadn't planned to write such a book, but from time to time various persons commented that this type of information could be valuable for others interested in knowing more about the park and its creation. Since I was intimately involved with Cama Beach and the park project and have written other books, I eventually realized I was an appropriate person to take on the commitment.

I tried to include perspectives in addition to my own by interviewing over forty persons. I also made an effort to mention others I'm aware of who were guests or workers at Cama Beach Resort or who helped in a significant way to turn the property into a park.

Still, to a large extent I wrote the narrative from my personal standpoint as a someone who grew up in the Stanwood-Camano area; who married one of the former owners and experienced the resort in operation during its final two decades; and who, as a lawyer with legislative experience at the State Capitol, later actively participated in the process of turning Cama Beach into a state park.

I'm grateful to my wife Sandra for many, many reasons. But of relevance to this book, I feel highly fortunate that I've had the privilege of becoming so involved with helping her and her sister Karen preserve their wonderful family heritage for the benefit of both present and future generations.

I would like to thank the many persons who took the time to be interviewed. I'm grateful to Karen Prasse, Bill Blandin, and the Stanwood Area Historical Society for many of the photographs and background materials. Also helpful with photos or graphics were David Pinkham at the *Stanwood/Camano NEWS*; Carol Triplett; Parametrix consulting architect Mark Van Vliet; Leavengood Architects; and State Parks staff, particularly Melanie Ford Bissey, Tina Dinzl-Pederson, and Catherine Rucker. And I greatly appreciate my proofreaders. The names of all those who helped are in the Acknowledgments section at the end.

I welcome comments from readers, who can reach me through my web site at www.GaryWorthington.com.

And now, I hope you enjoy reading about a truly unique and beautiful state park, which many people appropriately call "magical."

Gary Worthington
Olympia, WA
February 2007—May 2008

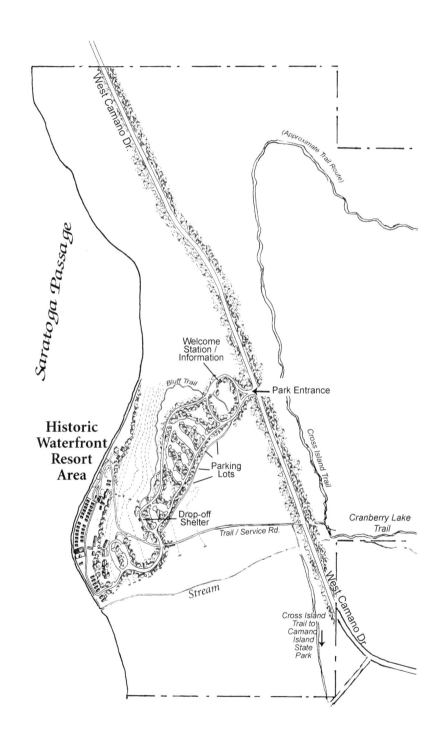

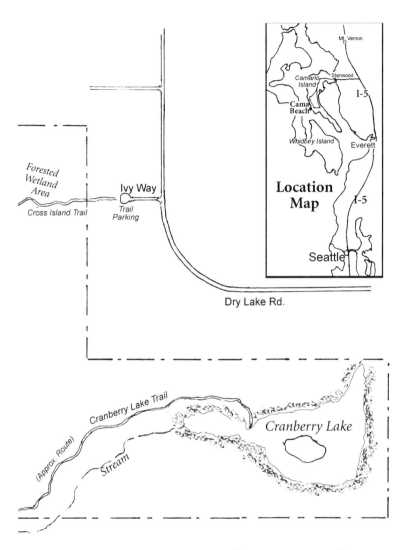

Forested
Wetland
Area

Cross Island Trail

Ivy Way

Trail
Parking

Dry Lake Rd.

Cranberry Lake Trail

(Approx. Route)

Stream

Cranberry Lake

Location Map

Mt. Vernon

Camano
Island

Stanwood

I-5

Cama
Beach

Whidbey Island

Everett

I-5

Seattle

Cama Beach State Park

N

0   1/4

Scale in Miles

A Camano Island Map is on Page 18

Mountain View Rd. W.

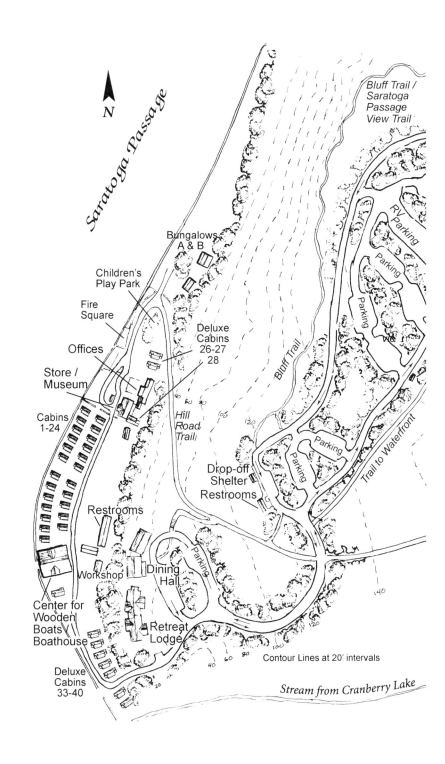

N

Saratoga Passage

Bluff Trail /
Saratoga
Passage
View Trail

RV Parking

Parking

Parking

Bungalows
A & B

Children's
Play Park

Fire
Square

Offices

Deluxe
Cabins
26-27
28

Bluff Trail

Store /
Museum

Cabins
1-24

*Hill
Road
Trail*

Parking

Parking

Trail to Waterfront

Drop-off
Shelter

Restrooms

Restrooms

Parking

Workshop

Dining
Hall

Center for
Wooden
Boats
Boathouse

Retreat
Lodge

Deluxe
Cabins
33-40

Contour Lines at 20' intervals

Stream from Cranberry Lake

40   60   80

20

100

120

140

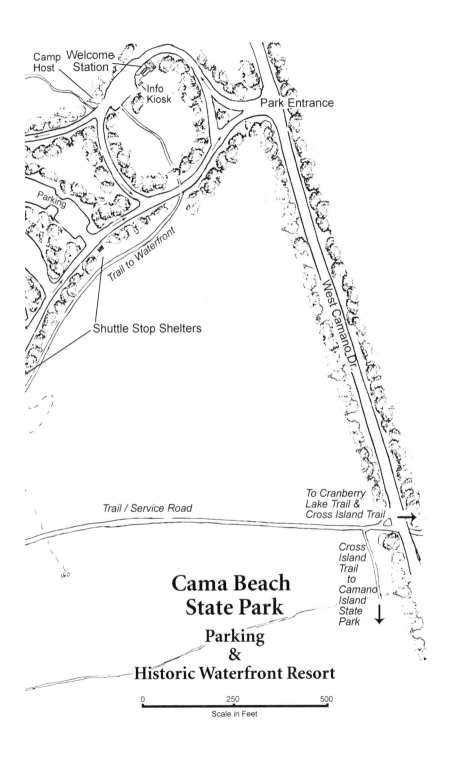

Camp Host

Welcome Station

Info Kiosk

Park Entrance

Parking

Trail to Waterfront

West Camano Dr.

Shuttle Stop Shelters

To Cranberry Lake Trail & Cross Island Trail

Trail / Service Road

160

Cross Island Trail to Camano Island State Park

Cama Beach State Park

Parking
&
Historic Waterfront Resort

0   250   500

Scale in Feet

A Brief Cama Beach Chronology

c.350 to 1800s	Seasonal camp and overnight site for Native Americans.
1880s to 1908	Logging camps
1933-34	LeRoy (L.R.) Stradley purchases land and constructs resort.
1934	Cama Beach Resort opens May 19.
1938	L.R. Stradley dies; daughter Muriel Stradley Risk and husband Lee R. Risk take over management.
1989	Cama Beach Resort closes after 55 years under same owners.
1990-91	Heirs approach Washington State Parks to propose a state park.
1991	The Center for Wooden Boats begins involvement.
1993	Friends of Cama, later Friends of Camano Island Parks formed.
1994 to 1998	Land acquisition by state through four phases of donations and purchases.
1997	Master Plan for State Park approved.
1998	Frank Galloway becomes Cama Beach State Park's first ranger.
1999 to 2006	Various project delays due to tribal concerns.
2001	Jeff Wheeler takes over as ranger and area manager.
2002 to 2006	Archaeological survey work in beach area
2003	Upland area parking lots, roads, and utilities constructed.
2006 to 2008	Construction of welcome station, parking lot restrooms, drop-off shelter, waterfront utilities; renovation of historic resort buildings.
June 21, 2008	Grand Opening. Historic resort cabins available for rental.
2009	Completion of Dining Hall and Retreat Lodge.

Introduction
THE CAMA BEACH EXPERIENCE

"This place has a magic to it," as former owner Sandra Risk Worthington observes, and as Park Manager Jeff Wheeler and countless others have felt over many years.

Perhaps this rare atmosphere is due, as Worthington believes, at least partly to the sense of remoteness. "It's about shutting out the busyness of everyday life, about getting away. As you leave Stanwood, the scenery gets more and more rural. Arriving at Cama Beach, you change your focus to what's natural—the woods and the waves. And the old resort itself doesn't try to impress you; it's the beauty of the setting that does."

Perhaps, as many guests say, part of the magic is also the feeling of an earlier time when life seemed less complicated.

And maybe the atmosphere is also due to somehow sensing the spirits of the Native American ancestors who frequented the site.

Whatever the explanation, the park is a place for nourishing our souls.

Visitors need to slow down, to make a place within themselves to experience and absorb the unique natural setting without the constant interruptions and distractions of the modern technological world.

This is an opportunity for *quiet* and for listening to the sounds of nature.

Turn off electronic devices. Put away earphones and earbuds. If you *must* check for electronic messages, do it infrequently, and do it in a place where other people won't notice.

Go for a walk on the beach. Examine the tiny shells and the variations in pebbles, the scent of the seaweed, the flamboyant shapes of the driftwood.

Walk on the many trails in the forest. Go slowly and pay attention to the details of your surroundings. Look at the tiny plants as well as the trees. Smell the scents of firs and of moist soil. Watch for other living creatures of all sizes.

If the night sky is clear, look at the stars. Take the time to appreciate the glories of the larger universe. The artificial lighting is deliberately kept low at Cama Beach, so guests can experience the dark.

Turn off television, music players, portable computers, electronic games.

Pay attention to what's going on around you *here*, not to what's happening somewhere else in the world.

Read the interpretive signs and look at the exhibits. Attend the talks and the nature walks. Ask questions of the trained staff and the docents, all of whom are glad to share their knowledge and experience.

Spend time with your family and friends. Introduce yourself to other visitors and get to know them. Cama Beach has always been a place that builds community and encourages being sociable.

The park depends on volunteers for much of its functioning. If you feel so inclined, approach the staff or a volunteer and ask how you can help, whether for a an hour or for years.

If you decide you need additional entertainment, read. Cama Beach has books and other worthwhile sources of information available. Learn something you otherwise wouldn't.

PART ONE

A BRIEF GUIDE TO THE PARK

Camano Island's Two State Parks

Camano Island has two major waterfront state parks (in addition to a number of smaller county parks). Each of the state parks has much to offer visitors, but the facilities and programs differ.

Camano Island State Park provides extensive campgrounds; a public boat launching ramp; large picnic areas; 6,700 feet of beach; a kitchen shelter by the waterfront; an amphitheater for interpretive programs; a group camp; five rental cabins; and 134 acres with nature trails. Visitors can drive directly to these facilities. The park was designated for public use in 1949. It is noted for its initial development in a single day by 900 local area volunteers.

Cama Beach State Park opened in June 2008. It offers a unique 1930s era resort listed on the National Register of Historic Places; thirty-six waterfront cabins available for rent; a branch campus of Seattle's Center for Wooden Boats with classes in boat building and handling as well as small wooden boats for rent; over a mile of beach with a limited waterfront picnic area; a small museum and gift shop; 434 acres with extensive nature trails; and a wide range of interpretive programs in outdoor education and the history of the site and the area. Beginning in 2010, Cama Beach will offer a dining hall with meals for both day visitors and overnight guests; a retreat lodge with fifteen rooms for overnight accommodations and meeting rooms; and mooring buoys and floats for boaters. The waterfront is a significant archaeological area due to its use as a seasonal Native American camping site for at least 1,600 years.

Unlike Camano Island State Park, at Cama Beach the public must park vehicles in the lots away from the waterfront. Visitors can then either walk down the steep hill to the historic beachfront resort area or ride in shuttle vehicles operated by the staff. Visitors with disabilities can be accommodated by asking the park staff. Cama Beach does not have camp sites or a public boat launch area. Guests can

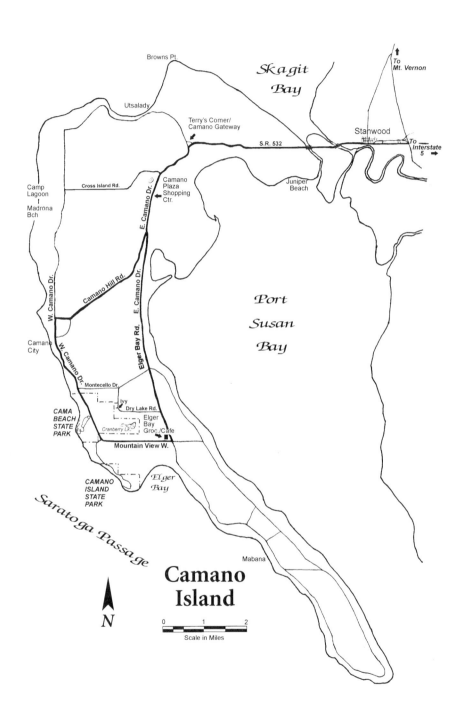

instead rent the waterfront cabins, and boats can be rented at The Center for Wooden Boats.

The information in this book is oriented toward Cama Beach, but details on Camano Island State Park are available by asking the staff at either park, as well as online through the web site at www.parks.wa.gov.

Finding Your Way on Camano Island

Island Transit provides free and frequent bus service directly to Cama Beach State Park. Details are at www.islandtransit.org, or phone toll free (800) 240-8747. If you are driving yourself or riding a bicycle, the distance is around 13 to 14 miles from Stanwood, depending on the route chosen.

Leaving Stanwood by highway heading west, visitors cross a narrow branch channel of the Stillaguamish River, then a smaller bridge over Davis Slough before continuing uphill onto Camano Island. The island is still largely rural in feel, with expanses of forest and farmlands, though there are increasing numbers of housing subdivisions, often screened by woods. Camano Island is roughly eighteen miles long from north to south, and it varies from one to seven miles in width.

Cama Beach State Park is on the southwest shore of the island, about two-thirds of the way down the island's length. The park faces Camano's larger sister, Whidbey Island, across Saratoga Passage.

To get to the park, after crossing onto Camano Island continue two miles to Terry's Corner, with its Camano Gateway sign and a small commercial area. Take the left fork of the highway and head south on East Camano Drive.

In another two miles or so, there is a choice of routes:

(1) *The East Camano Drive/Elger Bay Route*: For those who continue south on this slightly longer route (with a steep, long hill at the end to challenge bicyclists) it will be five miles before making any turns. During that distance East Camano Drive becomes Elger Bay Road.

Turn right (west) at the Elger Bay Grocery store and cross the island on Mountain View Drive. After a long climb, the main road turns right to become West Camano Drive (turning left at that point leads to Camano Island State Park). Continue another half mile to the entrance to Cama Beach State Park .

(2) *The Camano Hill Route*: For an alternate route, over a mile shorter, angle right to climb Camano Hill Road (the long upward grade might tire some bicyclists) and cross to the west side of the island. There, turn left (south) at the intersection with West Camano Drive and continue another three miles or so to Cama Beach State Park. The entrance to the park is on the right.

Arriving at Cama Beach

Entering the Cama Beach State Park boundary on West Camano Drive, it is immediately obvious that this is a special place. A mile wide expanse of shady, lush Northwest forest begins, mostly unchanged for the past seventy or more years.

After turning in at the gate in the middle of the park, visitors stop at the Welcome Station for a brief orientation. Then, most guests will continue on the entry road designed to offer a calm experience of light filtering through the trees from the sky over Saratoga Passage.

Welcome Station

To preserve the quiet ambience of an earlier era, visitors' cars are intentionally kept away from the historic resort area.

Drivers with vehicles to park are led by the road to the lot closest to the top of the steep hill above the waterfront. They may find it convenient to leave off passengers and belongings at the sheltered waiting area before doubling back to the parking bays, where the first available spot they see is likely to be the closest to their destination.

RVs and vehicles with trailers are accommodated in a signed parking bay with longer slots, closer to the Welcome Station.

Parking Area Drop-off Shelter

The parking areas are each named after one of the other former historic resorts on Camano Island, as a way of keeping alive the era when a dozen or more of these summer facilities operated (Cama Beach was the largest). A couple of additional small covered waiting areas are available next to lots farther away from the main Drop-off Shelter with its nearby restrooms.

If you are physically able and the weather cooperates, enjoy a leisurely walk down to the waterfront. Transportation is also available, typically in the form of a quiet electric vehicle or a larger shuttle van.

If you are arriving by boat, Cama Beach is unmistakable from either direction. The line of beach front homes ends, and over a mile of undeveloped shoreline is broken only by a flat point of land occupied by what appears to be a fishing village from an earlier era.

A Guide to the Historic Waterfront Area:

The park staff and docents are glad to answer any remaining questions about the site or its history.

The Hill Road. After Cama Beach Resort opened in 1934, guests arrived at the waterfront by driving down the straight, relatively steep gravel road near the north end. The roadway was originally a skid road for dragging logs down to the waterfront area when timber was harvested in the 1880s through the early 1900s. It is now used primarily as a walking path for access to the resort area and the beach.

Hill Road Path

The Waterfront Area – From Native American Use to Cama Beach Resort. The unique cultural importance of the resort area has earned listings on both the National Register of Historic Places and the Washington Heritage Register.

The level land on the waterfront has attracted visitors for at least two thousand years. Native Americans beached their canoes and camped on the site during the warmer seasons. They processed shellfish and fish near the beach, gradually building up an extensive midden of shells, fish bones, and animal bones that now lies deep beneath the surface.

Later, in the 1880s through the early 1900s, the area was a site for logging camps. The original forest was cleared, and the logs were dragged by horses down a skid road to the waterfront for loading onto ships.

In the early 1930s Seattle businessman L.R. Stradley began purchasing parcels of land. He eventually accumulated around 434 acres with over a mile of shoreline, which he named "Cama Beach." In 1934 he and his family opened Cama Beach Resort. After his death in 1938, his daughter and her husband, Muriel Stradley Risk and Lee R. Risk, who lived on the site year round, continued to operate the resort in the summers until 1989. Their two daughters, Karen and Sandra, grew up at the resort and worked there during the busy summer seasons.

From a Resort to a State Park. In 1990-91, these two daughters, Karen Risk Hamalainen and Sandra Risk Worthington, and their respective husbands Asko Hamalainen and myself, approached representatives of the Washington State Parks and Recreation Commission and initiated the process of turning the property into a state park. The family donated 60 per cent of the value of the 434 acre waterfront property as well as cash donations for a master plan for the park and for construction of the new Dining Hall/Commons Building. Public funds, mostly through legislative appropriations, paid for the remainder of the land acquisition and for the necessary development work including upgrading the utility systems and resort structures, several new buildings, and archaeological surveys.

At the instigation of the former owners and others, The Center for Wooden Boats (CWB) based at Seattle's Lake Union became a partner in the project from the beginning. Interested local citizens and members of groups such as Friends of Camano Island Parks and CWB lobbied the legislature for funds and helped maintain the property during the long process.

Key state legislators played crucial roles in obtaining the funding, led particularly by Senator Mary Margaret Haugen of Camano Island, from beginning to end. Representative Hans Dunshee of Snohomish and, in the earlier years, Representatives Barry Sehlin of Oak Harbor and Ed Murray of Seattle were also especially instrumental in ensuring appropriations for the park.

It took almost eighteen years of persistent efforts before the park was ready to be opened to the public. The latter half of this book recounts some of the main events in this process and provides some understanding of why it took so long.

Cama Beach Resort Buildings, c. 1950, from a Postcard *(Ellis photo #8110)*

The Beach. The gravelly beach and the waters of Saratoga Passage have been the obvious main attraction of the area throughout the thousands of years of Native American use and up to the present day. Fishing was a principal draw for decades when the resort operated. Cama Beach had a fleet of over forty small boats for guests to rent.

Tribal people, and later guests at the resort, dug for clams and other shellfish on the beach. Resort guests anchored crab pots (traps) offshore. Families walked along the beach and children played among the driftwood logs. The resort sponsored summer swimming classes which were popular despite the coolness of the waters. In later years, many guests brought their own boats and anchored them offshore.

Lucky visitors occasionally see orcas or gray whales in the distance.

The Sea Wall. This 2,100 foot long concrete bulkhead was built in the early 1950s over several years by Lee Risk and hired help. The wall was extended section by section at low tides during the

The Beach and Sea Wall

seasons when the resort was closed. The concrete barrier replaced the log bulkhead that can be seen in many early photos of the resort.

The Store. The store was in many ways the nerve center of Cama Beach Resort. Guests checked in and out there. They bought groceries, candy, soda pop and ice cream, and they checked out and rented fishing gear and sports and game equipment. Often they would hang around in the store to engage in conversation among

themselves and with the owners. Photos of guests and the fish they had caught were posted, along with various rules and other information which can still be seen on the walls. The manager's office was at the north end of the store area.

The store building is now used as a small information center, gift shop, museum, and office for the Beach Watcher docents and volunteers.

Store and Gas Pump

The Gas Pump Island. The gas pump, a prominent fixture in front of the Cama Beach store, was of an early design, with a long lever-like handle that was manually pivoted back and forth to pump the gasoline from an underground tank to the large glass cylinder chamber at the top. The glass was scored with horizontal lines to measure the amount of fuel being dispensed. The gasoline flowed downward by gravity from the glass cylinder chamber, through a hose with a nozzle and trigger at the end and into the vehicle or a container. The body of the pump, like the nearby lubricating oil dispensers, was painted green. A cylindrical air compressor adjacent to the gas pump was used primarily to inflate inner tubes for swimming use in the summers.

The current gas pump (not operable) and the oil dispensing equipment are replacements of approximately the same time period but with some minor differences in design.

The facility was an official Chevron service station for many decades, despite its relatively small size.

The House. Built in 1941, with a bedroom/playroom added on the north end around 1950, the house was the year round residence of the Risk family who owned and operated the resort. After rehabilitation, which included the removal of an enclosed porch addition connect-

The Owners' House (now offices).

ing the house to the store building, it now contains offices and meeting rooms.

The Fire Square. The small area enclosed by low rock walls was a gathering and conversation area, mainly in the evenings after a fire was built in the center. The wood burned was usually driftwood collected from the beach during the winters.

The Fire Square set up for a large picnic.

The Children's Play Area. The small play park with swings at the base of the main hill road was mostly surrounded by tall bushes—lilacs, wild roses, ocean spray, and snowberries—that made a good location for playing hide-and-seek. Throughout the period of the resort's operation the area contained a teeter-totter, swings, and a sand box.

The Waterfront Cabins. Although rehabilitated in 2007-2008, the waterfront rental cabins (also referred to by some former guests as "cottages" or "fishermen's cabins"), numbered 1 through 24, are very much as they were at the time of construction in 1933-34. Built in a short period of time during the Great Depression by a large crew of local men hired by L.R. Stradley, the cabins were rented out as

The Front Row of Waterfront Cabins

overnight accommodations. Normally a cabin held up to four guests, though a fifth could be added for an extra charge. These cabins had no bathroom facilities, so guests depended on the toilets and showers in the south end of the Recreation Hall until that building burned to the ground in 1977. Afterwards, two small outhouse type pit toilets were available. Since the number of guests had declined substantially, these were considered adequate by many.

The most obvious difference resulting from the rehabilitation of the cabins is that the cast iron, wood burning cook stoves have been removed, though microwaves have been added.

The sinks have been retained and refurbished. Both hot and cold water are now available at the sinks, with on-demand hot water heaters installed under the kitchen counters. The old ice boxes have been replaced by small refrigerators.

Kitchen in Waterfront Cabin

Electric wall mounted room heaters have also been added, as well as outlets for plugging in communications devices. The chimneys were removed and rebuilt with the same bricks to retain the original appearance, but they now are supported on new metal stanchions and no longer serve an actual function. The floors and ceilings have been insulated. However, due to the unusual horizontal stud method of construction, it was impractical to insulate the walls.

Each window was cleverly crafted with an attached screen. The edge-to-edge units slide into the wall cavities on each side, so opening a window also pulls its screen into position. However, the design meant it was not feasible to add another layer of glass to the windows for additional insulation.

The cabins have been raised an average of one to one-and-a-half feet above their original grade level to minimize possible impacts from flooding. They are on new pad and pier foundations, designed to avoid intruding upon any underlying archaeological deposits. Fill dirt was spread around the cabins, raising the ground level so as to maintain the overall historic appearance of the immediate area.

The Deluxe Cabins. These rental cabins, numbered 26 through 38, of which ten remain, are identical to the smaller waterfront cabins, except that a bathroom was later attached to the back of each of the "deluxe" cabins (Cabin 38 is different, with a large rear bedroom). The deluxe cabins were re-habilitated in 2007-2008 with the same modifications as the smaller waterfront cabins plus new bathroom fixtures and

Deluxe Cabins at South End

shower stalls. The addition of the on-demand hot water heaters also means hot showers are now readily available. Since it is no longer necessary to use wood stoves to heat hot water tanks, these stoves and tanks have been removed.

Employees at the resort often lived in Cabin 28 adjacent to the store and the house. Four deluxe cabins were originally on the site of the Retreat Lodge; three burned on the same day in the 1950s. The remaining Cabin 32 was dismantled during park development and its components used for renovation of other resort buildings.

The Center for Wooden Boats Buildings

The Boathouse. The fleet of forty or so Cama Beach boats was stored in the large Boathouse after the building was completed around 1950. The boats were lowered into the water and retrieved on a wheeled carriage traveling on steel rails. The carriage was pulled by a cable around an electric powered winch. A model at the boathouse illustrates how the railway worked.

The Boathouse is now operated by The Center for Wooden Boats (CWB) and used for boat rentals for the public, exhibits, and its own wide range of boating related programs. CWB educational offerings include classes for adults and youths in boat building, boat handling, and maritime history.

Boathouse under renovation by The Center for Wooden Boats.

Efforts are being made to replace the Marine Railway, which was no longer functioning by the time the resort closed.

The Boatman's House. The resort employee who handled the boats and his family lived in this cabin immediately to the south of the boathouse. The Boatman's House is now used as accommodations for CWB's instructors and others.

The Shop. Maintenance work on equipment and furnishings was done in the small workshop building, where tools were also stored. The shop is now part of CWB's facilities.

The Fire Truck Garage (now a classroom). The building across the roadway to the east of the Boathouse was originally a fire truck garage. The structure is now used by The Center for Wooden Boats, primarily for its classes, as well as being available for classroom use by others.

Mooring Buoys and Floats. Although not yet operating at the original opening date of the park, these facilities are expected to be available for use by both the boating public and by CWB.

The Ping Pong Pen (now Restrooms). This reconstructed building originally housed ping pong tables in the north half and a large storage area in the south half. The present exterior replicates the original building. However, the interior is now totally redesigned and rebuilt as a comfort station with toilets, sinks, and showers for use by occupants of the waterfront cabins and other park visitors.

The Recreation Hall and Tennis Court Site. To the south of the store, a fireplace and chimney made of river rocks and brick marks the eastern side of the former Recreation Hall which totally burned in 1977. This large building had a central meeting room where guests gathered in the evenings and in rainy weather for conversation, playing games, square dancing, and watching movies. The building also contained storage rooms, a laundry/utility room, and the toilets and showers for use by guests in the small waterfront cabins.

It is hoped that eventually the structure will be rebuilt, with the interior redesigned for current needs such as meeting and classroom space, restrooms, and a small coffee/snack shop.

Communications Building (formerly for storage), and Fireplace from former Recreation Hall

South of the Recreation Hall site is a level area which originally contained a concrete tennis court built in 1941 and surrounded by a high fence.

The Warehouse/Storage Building. The separate small building to the southeast of the store originally stored supplies for the resort. It now contains equipment monitoring and controlling the heating, sewage, and water systems at the park, as well as a microwave relay for communications.

The Bungalows. The bungalows were larger rental cabins on the northern portion of the resort area, each with its own bathroom and a fireplace. A bungalow normally accommodated up to six persons. Only two bungalows remain of the original ten, which were designated with letters from A through J, from south to north. Bungalow J at the far north end of the waterfront area was destroyed by a mudslide in the

Bungalows

1990s, and seven other bungalows were later dismantled due to their deteriorated condition. Materials were saved for use in repairs and renovations of other resort structures.

The two remaining bungalows, designated as A and B, are used for meetings and for overnight stays.

The Forest Trails. The trails in "Cama Woods" were used occasionally during the resort era, but the activities of most guests were focused on the waterfront area. The Friends of Camano Island Parks have now built and maintained an extensive trail system which park visitors are encouraged to use (please see the maps available at the park and in the front of this book).

The *Bluff Trail* or *Saratoga Passage View Trail* of around one-half mile parallels the bluff above the waterfront, connecting the Welcome Center and the Drop-off Shelter areas.

The *Cama Woods Trail* is part of the *Cross Island Trail* system. Around a mile, it connects the West Camano Drive area with Ivy Lane near the northeast corner of the park.

Another mile long section of the Cross Island trail connects Cama Beach State Park with Camano Island State Park, paralleling the county roads between the parks.

The *Cranberry Lake Trail* is around a mile and a quarter total, going and returning from its starting point off West Camano Drive. Information about the lake follows.

Cranberry Lake and the Stream. Resort guests rarely made the somewhat long hike through the forest to Cranberry Lake at the far eastern end of the Cama Beach property. Until houses were built on neighboring property to the east in the 1980s to 1990s, the boggy lake of around twelve acres was relatively remote, a peaceful haven for birds and other wildlife. Beavers built a lodge and dam, but they were apparently eventually killed by intruders with guns who also destroyed the dam. After an absence of many years the beavers have returned.

Cranberry Lake (*Photo by Tina Dinzl-Pederson, Cama Beach State Park*)

Over the past few decades the volume of water in the small stream that originates in the lake and flows through the ravine to the sound has varied from season to season. The freshwater previously fanned out into a little delta on the beach before entering the sound. However, in later years the stream typically disappears as it approaches the saltwater by seeping into the ground at the upper edge of the beach.

The trail to Cranberry Lake has now been renovated and maintained for public use by the Friends of Camano Island Parks. The lake is a quiet bird and animal sanctuary, so visitors are asked to keep to the designated trails and viewing areas.

The Night Sky. Few places in the urbanized Puget Sound basin are as free of artificial lighting as the Cama Beach property. To minimize illumination of the night sky, outdoor lights in the areas frequented by visitors have been intentionally designed to be directed downward and to provide only the amount of illumination needed for safety and for finding one's way. The vast majority of the 430-plus acres has no lighting, nor, of course, does the expanse of water between Camano and Whidbey Islands.

So whenever the night sky is clear, be sure to spend some time gazing at it, just as your ancestors did over the many millennia before artificial lights took over. You can see the Milky Way and thousands of other celestial features with only your eyes, but you should also consider using binoculars or setting up a telescope.

"Meteor showers" occur at certain dates throughout the year when the earth passes through areas of debris in space. Some major meteor showers, and their peak viewing dates, are the Lyrids (April 21-22), the Perseids (August 10-12), the Orionids (October 21), and the Geminids (December 13). Plan to lie down on your back in an open area or on the beach at these times, and see who can spot the most "falling stars."

Later Additions to the Park

The Welcome Station. The first building encountered by most visitors to the park provides orientation and information materials and displays, as well as guest reservation and registration facilities, and some gift items for sale. Completed in 2007, the Welcome Station's details and overall proportions are based on those of the historic Cama Beach Resort structures on the waterfront. The building was designed by architect Mark Van Vliet on behalf of the engineering and design consulting firm Parametrix, Inc., and built by Advanced Construction, Inc., of Mukilteo, WA. The stone work, designed in the same style as the older rock walls of the resort area, was done by mason Wayne Gagnon, of Marysville, WA.

Parking Lot Drop-off Shelter and Restrooms. The covered waiting area and the nearby comfort station at the edge of the main hill, completed in 2007, are intended primarily for use by park visitors awaiting transportation to the waterfront area or gathering for hikes or other activities. As with the Welcome Station, the structures were designed by Mark Van Vliet, AIA, on behalf of Parametrix, and built by Advanced Construction, Inc., of Mukilteo.

Drop-off Shelter and Stone Walls

The stone walls by the buildings are similar to the rock walls in the historic resort area, but for safety reasons, they were required to be higher than the walls at the resort. To minimize interference with views, they were designed by Parametrix landscape architects Curt Warber and Jens Swenson to be partly "transparent," with a gap between the rock at the bottom and the log rails at the top, similar to the old CCC-era walls built at some other parks. As with the stonework by the Welcome station, the walls were built by mason Wayne Gagnon of Marysville.

The Dining Hall/Commons. The Dining Hall provides meals for park visitors as well as space for public meetings and other events. Scheduled for completion in late 2009, the structure is designed by Leavengood Architects, Seattle. Construction funds were donated by the former owners of Cama Beach, through the Hamalainen Charitable Trust and the Worthington Foundation, facilitated by the Washington State Parks Foundation.

A different, larger version of this structure designed by Miller/Hull Architects, Seattle, had originally been intended for the site of the resort's former Recreation Hall near the waterfront cabins. However, the building's location was changed due to concerns about the foundation disturbing the underlying archaeological deposits.

Dining Hall *(Rendering by Leavengood Architects)*

The Retreat Lodge. The Retreat Lodge has fifteen guest rooms for overnight stays, each with its own bathroom, as well as meeting rooms and lounging areas for groups and individuals attending retreats, conferences, and events such as weddings and reunions. Scheduled for completion in late 2009, the building is designed by Leavengood Architects, Seattle. Construction was funded through Certificates of Participation (bonds authorized by the state legislature to be repaid, with interest, from rental fees charged for the use of the building).

Retreat Lodge *(Rendering by Leavengood Architects)*

Art Work at Cama Beach

The park houses a donated collection of high quality art pieces by well known Northwest artists. The walls of the rental cabins are decorated with a variety of historic Cama Beach photos.

In particular, don't miss the following art works (additional pieces will be added as the collection expands):

Painting, "The Grand Opening of Camano Island's World Famous Fishing and Recreational Attraction – CAMA BEACH RESORT in 1934", by Jack Gunter, Camano Island. In the Dining Hall. Donated by Karen Hamalainen.

Bronze otter sculpture, by Ross Matteson, Olympia, WA. In the Dining Hall. Donated by Sandra and Gary Worthington.

Painting of Northwest Indian baskets among the trees, by Jack Gunter, Camano Island. In the Retreat Lodge. Donated by Karen Hamalainen.

Painting by Jack Gunter, "The Grand Opening . . . CAMA BEACH RESORT in 1934." *(Permission Jack Gunter)*

Wall Light sconces with old Cama Beach Resort logo, designed by Architect Renee Boone, then of The Miller/Hull Partnership, Seattle. In the Dining Hall and the Retreat Lodge.

Print, "Eagle's Wing," by Mark Henderson, Vancouver Island, B.C. In the Retreat Lodge. Donated by Sandra and Gary Worthington.

Other Exhibits:

The Munro historic tool collection: Presented to Cama Beach by former long term Washington Secretary of State Ralph Munro, who grew up on Bainbridge Island, WA, this collection of antique tools belonged to his father.

PART TWO

THE NATIVE AMERICAN CENTURIES

The Area Prior to Human Occupation

Thousands of years ago during the last ice age, what is now Puget Sound was covered with glaciers that had advanced southward from Canada. The ice was as much as 3,400 feet thick, and its immense weight sank the earth's crust in many areas. Around 11,000 years ago, the last glacier began to retreat. As the area slowly warmed over centuries the ice receded, leaving broad channels through which waters flowed in and out from the ocean. The melting icebergs and the resulting water carried mud, sand, and gravel over the area. Sediments settled to the bottom and were later reshaped by waves and weather.

Eventually fish, orcas, and gray whales swam to and fro from the ocean to the channel, with some of the fish feeding on life that grew in the eel grass near the shore. Water birds fed on the smaller fish. Clams grew in the perfect conditions of the area bathed by the tides.

At what later became known as Cama Beach a flat area of beach grew. Inland at a higher elevation a lake eventually formed, fed mainly by springs but also by runoff from the rains that fell on the surrounding lands. From the lake's outlet a small stream flowed through an increasingly deep ravine until it reached the salt water. Everywhere except for the beach, trees flourished: red cedars, firs, hemlocks, maples, madronas, alders. The lake and stream provided homes for beavers and birds. The forest was home to deer, racoons, otters, rabbits, skunks, and more birds.

Extensive archaeological work from 2001 through 2006 by a Cascadia Archaeology team under the leadership of Randall Schalk has considerably increased the knowledge of the Native American use of the site.

From numerous samples of soil layers the archaeological team proposed an interpretation of the formation of the beach area. Charles Hodges of Cascadia Archaeology suggests that the stream at the south end deposited sediment, forming a fan. This fan obstructed the movement of sediment along the shore, creating a bar. The bar gradually curved northward and back to the shore, accompanied by a low gravelly ridge forming along the bar's length. Between the curve of the bar and the shore a small wetland formed, fed by groundwater.

The Local Native Americans, and How They Lived

Around 1,600 years ago, people began coming to the beach in their dugout wooden canoes. In that time long before any roads, the sea was the way most inhabitants traveled any significant distance beyond their homes.   The overall designation generally given in modern times to the native peoples of this area is Coast Salish.

The Kikialus or Kikialos, one of the four tribes now comprising the Swinomish Indian Tribal Community, occupied the drainage of the south fork of the Skagit River downstream from what is now Mount Vernon, as well as much of Camano Island. They often camped at Cama Beach, which they called *Ya-Lked*.

Ancestors of the Snohomish, currently included as part of the Tulalip Tribes, also had seasonal camps at the site, which they referred to as *WHEE-uh-PUHK-wuhb*, or "place with a small promontory."

Ancestors of the Upper Skagit Tribe, of the Stillaguamish Tribe of Indians, and of the Samish Indian Nation also frequented the spot.

On Camano, the major permanent villages were in the area of what is now Utsalady on the island's north end and Camp Lagoon on the northwest. Smaller year round settlements were likely at Brown's Point at the island's far north, Madrona on the northwest, the Camano City area on the central west coast (a couple miles north of Cama Beach), and Juniper Beach, near where the island abuts the mainland.

In the warmer seasons the Native Americans journeyed from their villages and halted at the Cama Beach site, camping for days, weeks, even months on the broad area near the lagoon. They fished for salmon and other fish, hunted seals, dug for clams, and some hunted deer. Food that was not eaten immediately was preserved by smoking the fish or meat in sheds or on pole racks with fires built underneath.

Each family group had customary areas for harvesting fish, and shellfish, and for gathering berries, roots, cedar and other necessities. The native peoples did not have concepts of land ownership as did the European settlers, though the habitual usage of certain areas by particular groups was respected by the others.

According to archaeologist Randall Schalk, trolling for salmon from canoes was likely not productive with the fishing equipment then available. No fish hooks or weights for nets have yet been found, and the site does not appear especially suited to fish traps, so it seems probable that most of the salmon was caught in traps on the Skagit or other rivers and brought to the site.

Women harvested blackberries, salmonberries, cranberries, salal berries, wild strawberries, and huckleberries, as well as digging the roots of bracken ferns and cattails. Berries typically were spread on mats or slabs of cedar bark and dried in the sun. String was made from nettle fibers.

Edible seaweeds were also harvested, particularly the grass growing in shallow waters that was later twisted into bundles, dried in the sun, and chewed.

When the sap was running, the people removed cedar bark in long strips, shredded it, and wove it into mats, baskets, and clothing, or used it for towels and padding.

Since it was hard, long work to bring down a standing cedar tree to use the wood, trees that had already fallen were used whenever possible. To deliberately fall a tree, one was usually chosen near the shore. The only tools available before the time of the white settlers were stone adzes and wedges, in addition to the use of fires to burn through the trunks.

Cedar boards were bent and fastened together with wooden pegs to make boxes and water buckets. Trays and bowls were carved from red alder and maple chunks. Baskets were made from cedar bark and roots, from maple and wild cherry bark, and from horsetail roots. The baskets and boxes were used for storage, as well as for cooking using stone boiling.

The people wove blankets on simple looms using dog wool, down feathers, fireweed fibers, and goat wool brought from the mountains.

In the evenings, the people would sit around their campfires and feast on the bounty they had harvested, telling stories of their ancestors and legends of how the land, the sea, and the animals had come to be. When their meals were finished, they would discard the shells and the bones.

After darkness had fallen, they would often look up at the blackness of the sky. Especially if the moon had not risen to bathe the sky with its brilliance, they would gaze at the multitude of glittering stars, and at the pale band of light that crossed the heavens, all gradually shifting position as the night progressed and as the seasons changed.

Occasionally, while the people were camped, someone would die. After the prescribed rituals the body would typically be interred inside the fringe of the forest above the reach of the sea. The earlier practice in the region, when the forests extended to the water's edge, was to wrap bodies in woven cedar blankets suspended between two trees. Bodies wrapped in blankets or in cattail mats were also placed in canoes mounted on posts. Much later, Christians introduced the idea of underground burials.

Before the return of the harsher winter weather, the people usually returned to their permanent home villages and to the warmth of the fires in their long houses.

The Impacts of the Explorers and Settlers of European Descent

An expedition led by Captain George Vancouver, with his Lieutenant Whidbey, explored the Camano Island area in 1792. The U.S. Exploring Expedition of 1838-1842 led by Lieutenant Charles Wilkes named the island McDonough's Island and named the strait on the west side "Saratoga Passage." In 1847, the British named the island "Camano" in honor of Spanish Lieutenant Don Jacinto

Caamano, who never actually visited the island, but who had earlier explored the Nootka Sound waters around Vancouver Island.

In the first half of the nineteenth century, European settlers began arriving in larger numbers and claiming land for farms and other uses. To minimize conflicts, in 1855 the territorial and federal governments called a meeting of representatives of the regional native tribes at Mukilteo. The parties signed the Treaty of Point Elliott, which allowed those of European descent to claim ownership rights to most of the land in the area. In exchange, reservations were established as permanent homelands for the tribes, who were promised hunting and fishing rights in their "usual and accustomed" places, and schooling and medical services.

Over the following decades, the Native American use of traditional areas on Camano Island continued. Some tribal members worked at the steam-driven saw mill established at Utsalady in 1857. Native Americans also sold various trade items to the non-Indian workers and residents. In the early 1900s a couple of Kikialos and their wives lived at Camano City, working in logging camps and for farmers. Indian women are said to have knitted socks that were sold in the store at Camano City and widely worn.

Gradually, as the white settlement spread, the Native American usage of traditional sites on the island declined, including the area which became Cama Beach.

Archaeology at Cama Beach

Much of what is now known of the Native American presence at Cama Beach is based in part on the findings of the recent extensive archaeological work at the park. A mid-20th century survey under the auspices of the University of Washington labeled the site as "45IS2," and it was known at that time that an extensive shell midden lay under the ground. In 1995, a cultural resources survey confirmed that a late prehistoric shell midden underlies much of the historic Cama Beach Resort.

A 2002 report by Randall Schalk of Cascadia Archaeology summarizing testing in the spring of that year, says that "the site consists of a complex mosaic of both intact and disturbed cultural deposits as well as non-cultural sediments."

Radiocarbon dating showed that in the central portion of the waterfront area the oldest human occupation was between 1,000 and 1,640 years ago. The youngest portion of the waterfront appears to be in the northern area, which may mean that the southern portion was the first available level area for use by humans, and the useable area gradually

Figure 4.1 Illustration of: a) fine-grained basaltic unpatterened bipolar flake tool (Cat. # 2-3410 ST), b) basaltic lanceolate-shaped biface (Cat. # 2-3461), and c) fine-grained metasediment biface (Cat. # 2-3447 ST)

Stone scraping tools found at Cama Beach site. *(Illustration by Michael Wolverton, Cascadia Archaeology)*

extended northward. The convenience of fresh water from the stream may also have helped induced use of the southern area. The summary states, "Still older occupations in the southern portion of the resort may have been located on unstable surfaces" and are therefore no longer intact.

The most abundant stone artifacts are cooking stones, and "many of these exhibit contraction fractures . . . ." They were possibly used for "stone boiling, steaming clams, smoking fish, or simply heating the inside of a shelter."

According to Dr. Schalk, several hundred tiny stone beads were found near the former tennis court area. In front of the store, a large grooved stone was found, most likely a canoe anchor.

The remnants of marine species found, such as salmon, anchovies, and herring, varied from area to area, as did shellfish and mammal remains.

The main activities at the site appear to have been fishing and shellfish collecting. There was a wide range in both size and species of fish, and one possible explanation is that a tidal trap fishing technique may have been used. A fragment of a harpoon was found. The most common fish remains were staghorn sculpin, flatfish, salmon, perch, and buffalo sculpin bones.

Bird remains were mainly ducks and grebes. The relatively few mammal bones found included deer, elk, dog, harbor seal, and harbor porpoise.

Indications are that the site was occupied primarily in the spring, summer, or fall, but grebe and herring bones found might indicate some harvesting of those species in the winter. The report states that "the overall patterning of features, fauna, and artifacts seems consistent with the interpretation of the site as a seasonal resource collecting camp." A June 2005 updated summary points out, "The site

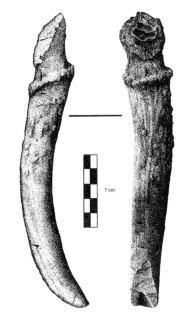

Figure 4.9 Illustration of antler artifact (Cat. # 2-4455 ST).

Antler scraping tool, found at Cama Beach site. *(Illustration by Michael Wolverton, Cascadia Archaeology)*

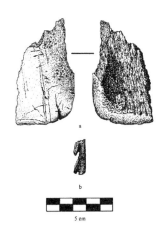

Figure 4.8 Illustration of: a) antler wedge (Cat. # 2-3298 ST). b) unilaterally barbed point fragment (Cat. # 2-4473 ST).

Antler wedge woodworking tool, and harpoon fragment, found at Cama Beach site. *(Illustration by Michael Wolverton, Cascadia Archaeology)*

may have been used at virtually any season as a way station for canoe travel between other residential and resource harvesting locations."

Remnants were found suggesting "the presence of structures such as temporary shelters or drying racks." However, no evidence was found of large structures in the test excavations, which were in the locations planned for utility trenches and other development work for the state park.

A fragment of an antler wedge and other tools suggested that woodworking activities may have taken place at the site.

However, many questions remain unanswered, such as the nature of the activities that went on in addition to harvesting and processing fish and shellfish, the fishing methods used, and the extent to which habitable structures were prevalent on the site.

PART THREE

THE LOGGING YEARS

Logging on Camano Island

It is probably difficult for most of us to imagine the extent to which the early settlers of European descent, and the Native Americans before them, depended on the sea for travel. Although the road networks of the white settlers gradually spread, boats plying Puget Sound were a major means of transport for many local people even into the 1920s and 1930s.

Until it closed in 1891 the major sawmill on Camano Island was at Utsalady on the north end. Over a couple of decades the entire island was inexorably stripped of its old growth forest. Trees were cut by hand sawing and by axes. For much of the period, until steam powered "donkey" engines came into use, horses and oxen were used to drag the logs out of the woods. Dragging was made easier by "skid roads": small, short logs placed on the ground across the roadway and typically greased. The tree trunks being pulled could then be slid over the tops of the logs on the ground with much less friction than if the trunks were dragged directly on the earth. Tall masted sailing ships carried spars for masts and lumber milled at Utsalady to San Francisco and other markets.

Logging at Cama Beach

Cama Beach was the location of English Logging Company's Camp 2, which closed operations around 1896. The steep hill road that was later the main entrance to the resort area was at first a skid road built for dragging logs down to a mill pond. Little is known about the details of the logging camp. Typically these facilities had a cookhouse and bunkhouses for the men. Loggers usually remained on the site rather than going home at night, since roads were scarce and travel was slow.

Esary logging crew with horses on a skid road at the site of the future Cama Beach hill road. *(Courtesy Amaryllis Whitmarsh, and collection of the Stanwood Area Historical* Society)

Esary logging crew at the future site of Cama Beach. Note the buildings in the background. *(Courtesy Amaryllis Whitmarsh, and collection of the Stanwood Area Historical Society)*

Esary logging crew at the future site of Cama Beach. Note the skid road area.
(Courtesy Amaryllis Whitmarsh, and collection of Stanwood Area Historical Society)

The mill established in 1905 at Camano City (a couple of miles north of the future Cama Beach) became the largest on the island. After the English Logging period, Tom Esary, who owned 300 acres of land around Camano City, ran a logging camp from 1905 to 1908 at Cama Beach. Esary was the largest logging operator on the island in that period, with a big camps also at Utsalady and Madrona. As Esary logged the area around Camano City he divided it and sold lots.

The Esary Logging Camp at Cama also had a skid road area at the shore, where the logs were put into the water to be towed by boats to the sawmill.

Life on Camano Island in the 1890s through 1930s

In the decades before establishment of its many resorts, life on Camano was similar to that on other inhabited Puget Sound islands. With the old growth forest entirely logged and much of the land cleared, small farms appeared. The island was at first an open range, where cattle could wander unrestrained, but little-by-little the farmers fenced their lands.

Although the dirt roads were gradually extended and improved, there was still frequent travel by water. A mail boat came daily to the dock at Camano City, where there was a post office. The community of Mabana, around four miles south of Cama Beach, also had a post office and a dock. A little ferry operated hourly between Utsalady on Camano and Oak Harbor on Whidbey Island from 1925 until 1936, when the Deception Pass bridge opened, providing direct highway access to Whidbey.

Small schools operated at Camano City, Elger Bay, and Mabana (the tiny school building still exists off the west side of West Camano Drive). Nels Bodin, who was born in 1922, began school at Camano City. He remembers that "you could count the number of students on your fingers." Until 1909, when a bridge was built connecting the island to Stanwood, a cable ferry was used to cross the slough.

With the improvement of the road links, regular boat traffic ceased. The post offices closed, and the island was served by a mail route from Stanwood. The island schools were closed in the late 1930s, after which children traveled by bus to Stanwood to attend school. It would be seventy years before elementary schools were again established on Camano.

Sawmills no longer operated on the island, so there was only occasional logging. After the advent of tugboats, log booms being towed to mills in Everett and elsewhere were a common sight off Cama Beach into the 1960s and even later. Gradually the convenience of transport by trucks made the log booms less common.

PART FOUR

THE RESORT YEARS

The history of Cama Beach in the 20th and 21st centuries is to a large degree the result of inspired visions—examples of what dedicated and creative individuals can do when they devote themselves to the common good. This was true of the original founding of Cama Beach Resort by L.R. Stradley, and of the operation of the resort for many decades by the founder's daughter and son-in-law, Muriel Stradley Risk and Lee Risk. It was also true of their heirs' long quest to perpetuate public use of the property by converting it to a major state park, as detailed in the latter half of this book.

The Building of Cama Beach Resort

The world of the 1930s through the 1960s was quite different in many ways from the world of the 21st century. Radio was the only electronic mass entertainment until the 1950s when television became common. Letter writing and land line telephones were the usual ways for long distance communication. Families and friends spent more time in face to face conversation and in activities such as playing board games or cards.

Typically, most families with a healthy wage earner could afford at least one car. But with few travel trailers or recreational vehicles, vacationers stayed in motels or pitched tents in campgrounds, or they went to cabins on the water or in the woods.

Only people who lived by the water or were ardent fishermen were likely to own a boat before the 1950s or so. But salmon and other fish were abundant in

Puget Sound, and almost anyone with a little instruction, minimal gear, and a rented boat could be successful at catching fish.

In this milieu, simple, rustic summer resorts were the venues for many family vacations. For a relatively low price, the resorts provided cabins or tenting areas; cooking facilities; stores selling food, beverages, and fishing gear; boats for rent; and if the resort were large enough, organized recreational activities.

These facilities are often referred to by historians as "auto court" or "motor court" resorts. However, those terms seem misleading if applied to Cama Beach, and they were never used by the Cama Beach owners or patrons. Although most users did arrive by car, the automobiles were parked by the cabins, and the use of the vehicles was then relatively infrequent. Many guests did not drive again until leaving at the end of their stay. The main resort activities were focused on the beach and the saltwater. Cama Beach was most often called a "family fishing resort," so that is how it is characterized in this book.

There are said to have been as many as twenty resorts on Camano Island in the 1930s through the 1940s, although some were small with their operations limited to renting a few cabins. Information about the resorts with many photos can be found in the book *Camano Island*, by Karen Prasse and the Stanwood Area Historical Society (Arcadia Publishing, 2006).

Cama Beach was the largest of the Camano Island resorts.

L.R. Stradley, Founder of Cama Beach Resort

Cama Beach Resort began as the inspiration of Seattle businessman Le-Roy Stradley. Mr. Stradley envisioned a resort on the water where ordinary families could vacation at relatively low cost. This principle was to guide the owners throughout the fifty-five years of the resort's operation. To a large extent it also guided the later vision for the public park.

Cama Beach Resort's founder. L.R. Stradley.

LeRoy Stradley was born in Iowa in 1879 and came to Seattle with his parents. He eventually owned a shipping newspaper, the *Daily Index*. The letterhead of correspondence he sent in 1935 lists himself as publisher also of *Index Shippers Guide, Index Passenger Guide, Shippers Travelers Guide,* and *Parcel Post and Mail Guide.* He formed Pacific The-

The Stradley family of Seattle, pre-Cama Beach. Left to Right: Lucy Stradley; daughters Iverne and Muriel, LeRoy (L.R.) Stradley.

atres Corporation and was the president of it for several years. In addition to owning theaters, he had numerous other real estate holdings.

Referred to by others as "Mr. Stradley," he signed himself as "L. R. Stradley" on all correspondence.

Mr. Stradley and his wife Lucy raised two daughters, Muriel and Iverne, in the family home at 117 Galer Street on Queen Anne Hill in Seattle (the house still exists at that address). Lucy Stradley handled the bookkeeping for the businesses. When she was old enough, Muriel handled much of the secretarial work and advertising. It would be Muriel, and her husband Lee Risk, who became the key family members involved in running Cama Beach Resort.

Cama Home, c. 1930s. The house had extensive grounds, with a large orchard, a goldfish pond, and a low stone perimeter wall. *(Courtesy Mike Dillon, and Stanwood Area Historical Society)*

Stradley owned land on Ericson Island near Milltown, north of Stanwood, which was a busy log mill location frequently visited by steamboats. During summer fishing expeditions to Ericson Island, the Stradleys discovered Camano Island.

L.R. Stradley soon purchased a house on the bluff overlooking the sound at Camano City, which he called "Cama Home."

The Cama Beach Land is Purchased

Mr. Stradley also soon began acquiring the property that would become Cama Beach Resort. With the exception of a couple of parcels east of the county road, the land was purchased by L.R. Stradley by means of a warranty deed dated July 12,

1933, from Elizabeth Frye Bogue and her husband Virgil N. Bogue. The price appears to have been slightly under $6,000.00 for the entire acreage west of the county road, including the mile plus of waterfront, and also for the majority of the pieces east of the county road, including Cranberry Lake.

On that same date, an assignment by the Bogues of real estate contracts, originally from the State of Washington to Herman W. Falk, gave Mr. Stradley the control of the abutting tidelands. This sale of the tidelands was finalized by a deed dated October 9, 1933, from the state to Mr. Stradley in consideration of $1,153.75.

On March 5 and March 9, 1934, a 40 acre parcel west of Cranberry Lake was deeded to Stradley from Gilbert S. and Maria Olsen, and by Maurice and Stella Reardon, respectively, thereby filling in a gap between parcels already purchased. And on April 7th, 1934, Stradley was the high bidder on a 20 acre piece abutting his northeast parcels, auctioned for nonpayment of taxes.

At that time only dirt roads served the island. Steamboats ran between Seattle and Mount Vernon, stopping at Mabana, Madrona, and Utsalady, and apparently at Cama Beach upon request.

The Resort's Construction

According to life long area resident Nels Bodin, much of the lumber for the construction of the resort was purchased in Stanwood, loaded onto a barge, and towed by boat to the beach. The lumber was offloaded and piled for later use. Mr. Bodin's father was hired to keep an eye on the building materials so they wouldn't be stolen. He and Nels, who was around eight or nine years old at the time, spent the summer living in a tiny cabin that had sometimes been occupied by commercial clam diggers. Nels Bodin remembers that the old skid road from Camano City to Cama Beach was not usable except possibly by Model T Fords, which were "long legged and light." The easiest access was by water until the road was improved.

Horse drawn grader used in leveling at Cama Beach. *(Stanwood Area Historical Society, 2002_57_140)*

Mr. Bodin remembers that Mr. Stradley wanted the beach to be the nicest one on Puget Sound, so Stradley had his crew wire together bundles of the driftwood logs that littered the beach. The driftwood was towed out to the middle of the sound by an outboard motor boat and released. But in the winter when Mr. Stradley came back, he found that more logs had floated in, even among the cabins, so he had to give up the idea of a perfectly clean beach.

Early construction work at Cama Beach, c. 1933. *(Stanwood Area Historical Society, 2002_57_127)*

Cama Beach Resort was built by a large crew that included long time Camano resident Ole Eide, as well as Stradley's future son-in-law, Lee R. Risk, who handled the payroll. Stradley's daughter Muriel was present for the construction, and it's likely that she participated in at least some aspects of the work.

According to Muriel Risk as quoted in the Stanwood News of January 28, 1971, the only building left from the logging era was the office, though the mill pond and log chute were still in existence. A Bridal Veil rose bush in the bungalow area also remained from earlier years.

A man named Shorty Russell handled the horses during the clearing. Other local men employed included H.V. Thompson, John Johnson, and John Ostraat. The crew filled in the log pond and marshy areas, leveled the ground, and built the

Cama Beach Resort under construction, c. 1934. *(Stanwood Area Historical Society, 2002_57_119)*

cabins. L.R. Stradley's cousin, Wilbur Stradley, had charge of the shop and other activities. The employment must have been welcome, given the depressed economy of those years.

A piece in the *Farm Bureau News* of Oak Harbor dated October 12, 1933, described the project:

> CAMANO CITY — Cama Beach is the scene of great activity these days. The beautiful new camp is being built in record time. Mr. Stradley has added new men to his force and work is being pushed as rapidly as possible. . . .
>
> The Cama Beach water system now has 3000 feet of main laid . . . Six bungalows have been completed. . . .
>
> Seventeen of the fifty cabins are finished and work is going steadily forward on the others.
>
> Two thousand feet of water front has been graded and planted to lawn which is already showing green . . . Work will start immediately on the general store, banquet hall, bath house, laundry, boat sheds and boat shop.
>
> Ernest Garrison has planned and supervised the construction of the water works.

A column in the *Twin City News* (later the *Stanwood News*, and later still the *Stanwood/Camano News*) dated October 12, 1933, provides an account of a visit to the site and some observations about the project's effects:

> I was down to the New Cama Beach Sunday. I was surprised to see what had been done there. . . . A road is being hewn from Campbell's corner. . . When I saw what Mr. Stradley had accomplished I wondered at his nerve and his apparent faith in the island and in the future of the Twin City neighborhood. Cama Beach is only one of Mr. Stradley's activities toward the development of the island. He has built himself a lovely house at Camano, a regular show place.
>
> He has charge of Cama Craft north of Camano and several other projects are under development. . . .
>
> Prosperous as we are here, we have to be led by outside capital. Some way an outsider can see a bigger perspective of our possibilities better than we can ourselves. . . .
>
> While Mr. Stradley is a Seattle man he buys everything he can in the Twin Cities. All his lumber, we understand, was brought from one of the local yards. Local labor is employed also. . . .
>
> . . . He is advertising the island extensively. All over Seattle one can see evidence of his work along this line. "

A March 22, 1934, piece under the Camano City heading in the *Twin City News* describes a visit to the site by air:

> Hundreds of people from far and wide have already come via land and water to inspect the finest fishing and recreational resort in the northwest, Cama Beach as it is rapidly nearing completion. . . . The honor of the first visitors to come to Cama by air fell to Mr. and Mrs. Steel and daughters of Seattle. Mid-afternoon of

March 17, they dropped from the clouds in the Eikorsky, an amphibian plane. They made a perfect landing on Cama Bay and taxied up onto the beach."

Prior to the May 1934 opening, the *Twin City News* said that forty "cottages" had been constructed. A May 17, 1934, headline in the *Twin City News* read, "Cama Beach to Open Saturday: New $150,000 Resort to Be Thrown Open to The Public." The piece stated in part:

> A new road has been cut through the forest to the beach, and while it is not as yet in tip-top shape, it is easily passable. Just drive south from Camano [City] and keep driving until you reach the beautiful waterfront . . . . Tons and tons of earth have been moved in the preparation for these grounds and tons and tons of material have been brought to the site. The opening of this resort is the beginning of a new day for Camano Island and this community should interest itself in what is going on there.

Cama Beach Resort Opens

The entries in Cama Beach Resort's Visitor Register book began on Saturday, May 19, 1934. The first guests to sign were Mr. & Mrs. A. Stone of Denver Colorado, referred by the Roosevelt Hotel of Seattle. Although the majority of the guests that day were from Seattle, several local persons also signed the register the first few days.

A similar pattern followed in the ensuing weeks, with the majority of visitors from Seattle, but also a scattering from Bellingham, Everett, Mount Vernon, Tacoma, Spokane, and Vancouver, B.C. Given that travel took so much longer in those days, it's notewor-

First Page of the Cama Beach Resort Visitors' Register, 1934

thy that guests the first season also came from Los Angeles, Oakland, San Francisco, and even from Montana, Oklahoma, Ohio, and Missouri.

A *Twin City News* headline dated May 24, 1934, said, "Rain Keeps Many Away From Stradley's Opening." The body of the piece went on to say, "But the rain did not dampen the ardor of the Stanwood Commercial club, which sent a delegation . . . They were surprised by the work represented."

Lee Risk and Muriel Stradley were married that August. L.R. Stradley was listed on the first brochures as "Managing Owner," with Lee R. Risk under him as "Manager." The address for the resort was shown as Route 1, Stanwood, and the phone number as "104 R 4." The Seattle Office for the resort was the same as that of the *Daily Index*, at 84 University Street, with a phone number of MAin 3223.

With L.R. Stradley's strong personality and entrepreneurial spirit, the first few years of the resort operations would have been conducted exactly as he prescribed and in accordance with his vision for the property. Around 1936, Mr. Stradley and his wife Lucy moved from their home on Queen Anne Hill in Seattle to live permanently at Cama Home at Camano City.

Forrest Hopkins, a long time Camano resident, worked as boatman soon after the resort opened. At that time the boats were hauled on a long cable to the storage area at the rear near the bluff. Once when Hopkins was operating the winch, the cable snapped, lashing his foot and tearing off part of a toe. Illustrative of a very different atmosphere from the 21st Century, Hopkins afterwards wrote a letter to Mr. Stradley apologizing for the incident!

L.R. Stradley and Mickey. *(Stanwood Area Historical Society, 2002_57_143)*

Another incident involving Hopkins' dog Mickey illustrates L.R. Stradley's forceful personality. When Hopkins left to work in Alaska for a period, he arranged to leave the dog in Mr. Stradley's care. Upon Hopkins' return, Stradley, who had grown attached to Mickey, refused to give him back, and Hopkins accepted the change in ownership without argument.

The Untimely Death of the Founder

In April 1938, Mr. Stradley died suddenly of appendicitis. His family and the others involved in the resort were stunned by the sudden loss.

Muriel and Lee Risk took over sole management. The Risks operated the resort until it closed in 1989.

Stradley's widow Lucy spent the remaining years of her life at Cama Home. That house eventually became the family home of granddaughter Karen Risk Hamalainen, her husband Asko Hamalainen, and their two boys Michael and Brian. Cama Home was sold in 2004 to Mike and Carol Dillon. The new owners remodeled it while striving to maintain the home's original feel and character.

Sign for waterfront tracts for sale by L.R. Stradley, 1930s.

Stradley had also owned numerous other pieces of real estate on Camano and scattered around central Puget Sound. Some of them were traded or sold when the Cama Beach property was pieced together, but others remained in family ownership through the 1970s. The largest was a 50 acre piece the family called "Cama Heights" on a bluff north of Camano City.

The resort continued to be managed as L.R. Stradley would have wished, providing low cost accommodations and activities for ordinary families on summer vacations. Although some changes were made in the resort's layout, the most obvious being the addition of the boathouse and sea wall in the early 1950s, the overall outward appearance changed very little over the years.

The Resort in Operation

Muriel and Lee Risk

Cama Beach exists as it is today in large part because of Muriel and Lee Risk's tenacity in keeping the property intact for over fifty years with relatively few changes in the original resort buildings or their arrangement.

Muriel Stradley was born August 21, 1907, and spent her childhood in Seattle. She graduated from the University of Washington. She and future husband Lee Risk were both present at Cama Beach from the beginning of the construction in 1933 and were married in 1934. She greatly admired her father L.R. Stradley and was shocked by his sudden death in 1938. Although her mother, Lucy Stradley, continued to live three miles away at Cama Home, Lucy's participation in the resort operation was minimal, with the exception of the World War II years when her help was needed since Lee Risk was often gone.

Muriel and Lee Risk were fairly coequal managers of the resort business for most of its operational period, from the 1930s through at least the 1970s. Muriel handled most of the work taking reservations, checking in guests, and attending to their needs, as well as writing the text of the brochures and rate sheets.

In later years, Muriel took over more and more of the resort management. She

Muriel Stradley Risk *(Stanwood Area Historical Society, 2002_57_212)*

was a strong personality, and for many guests it's likely she came to personify the resort experience to a large extent. She was passionate about issues such as protecting both private property rights and the natural environment and was an early advocate of limiting population growth. She posted bumper stickers for the

latter cause on the walls of the store at Cama Beach, along with many other items such as old fishing photos and rules of conduct for guests.

Lee R. Risk was born June 2, 1908, in Butte, Montana. He graduated from Seattle's Roosevelt High School and then from the University of Washington as an accounting major. During much of his life, he kept the account books for the resort operation. During World War II, he regularly rode his motorcycle into Everett to work at the shipyard.

The Risks had two daughters: Karen, born in 1944, and Sandra, born in 1947. Both daughters would eventually be crucially important in Cama Beach becoming a state park.

Muriel and Lee Risk were adventurous. In 1938 they went on a long cruise on a freighter through the South Pacific.

Lee Risk *(Stanwood Area Historical Society, 2002_57_179)*

They skied in the winters until middle age, and they traveled widely to other areas of the U.S. and to the Caribbean. The family sometimes befriended foreign students attending the University of Washington or the local high school, and they later visited the students and their families on travels in Europe.

On the beach, left to right: Muriel Stradley Risk, daughter Karen, Archibald (Jock) Lindsay, Lee Risk. The Risks met Lindsay, of Edinburgh Scotland, on a freighter in the South Pacific.

How Cama Beach Resort Operated

Each year, Muriel Risk mailed brochures printed on goldenrod colored paper to the list of guests, almost always identical except for any changes in prices.

At the beginning of each season, Lee Risk made up a chart for recording the reservations, so that the managers could see at a glance the party's name, the type of accommodation, and remaining vacancies. Reservations were taken by phone and mail. Muriel typed the letters confirming the reservations on her old manual typewriter. Daughters Karen and Sandra remember many dinners interrupted by the phone ringing with guests calling for reservations, or else arriving and needing to be checked in.

Directional arrows to Cama Beach were a common site on area roads.

Muriel Risk typically checked in the guests upon their arrival. The resort kept a receipt book, and the individual reservation card was put in a pigeonhole behind the office desk for the appropriate cabin or bungalow. A peg board in the store was used for keeping track of items that were checked out to guests, such as shower keys or sporting equipment.

Guests parked their cars next to their own cabins, and in those days the cars were seldom used again until the guests left at the end of their stay.

Barbara Cook of Olympia recalls from her family's stays in the 1970s, "We always stayed in the waterfront units. The cabin was the closest we'd ever been to the water." The kitchens were furnished with cooking utensils, including enamel ware, and with drinking glasses, and with ceramic plates and cups from a restaurant supply company. "The dishes and cutlery were an assortment that might have come out of our grandmother's kitchen but carefully accounted for at check in and check

Front and back of the orange brochures mailed every year. This one is from 1982, after the resort stopped renting boats.

out by Mrs. Risk. The furniture was sturdy wood, made to last many lifetimes and looking as though it had.

"The small front porch provided shade and outdoor shelter . . . a place for board games in the daytime, and singing in the evening. Jerry Harper was quite a guitar player and we all loved to sing."

The smaller cabins in the two waterfront rows lacked hot water heaters, so it had to be heated in a kettle on the wood burning stove. Karen Hamalainen's impression is that the guests generally liked cooking meals on the wood stoves, though it could get smoky and hot at times. Barbara Cook says of her initial visit: "A wood cook stove? I'd never seen one and certainly didn't know how to make it work, let alone cook with it!" But, "Conrads were Cama Beach veterans and showed us the ropes. I learned to cook a decent meal on that wood stove and enjoyed playing house in that rustic cabin, feeling very much the pioneer. One year Joan Conrad even baked a birthday cake in the oven!"

These cabins had no showers, so a key had to be obtained from the store for access to showers in the Recreation Hall (after that building burned in 1977, showers were no longer available for the small cabins).

Milk and basic groceries were sold at the resort store, as well as soda pop, candy, and ice cream. Guests could run a tab at the store and pay for their purchases upon checking out at the end of their stay.

The deluxe cabins and bungalows had their own bathrooms, and they also had hot water tanks that were heated by pipes circulating the water through the stoves.

There were rules regarding the number of visitors allowed, mainly to preserve a pleasant environment for the guests. Some examples: four persons were allowed in a cabin for the basic rental fee, but there was an extra charge for a fifth guest. Six persons were allowed in a bungalow, with additional charges for each additional one. Day visitors were charged fifty cents.

Registration cards from the resort, 1951-52

The Guests

Guests at the resort frequently rented cabins for a week or longer. Often families would come during same time period each summer, when they knew other guests who had become friends would also be present. Families often came for many years. In some cases, guests who had come as children later brought their own children to stay, so three or more generations of a family might share Cama experiences and memories.

Relaxing by the beach, 1930s *(Stanwood Area Historical Society, 2002_57_020)*

Medical doctors who were regular guests liked the fact that they could not easily be reached by telephone. There was only one phone for public use, behind the office desk in the store building. In earlier years the phone, on a multiparty line, had the number West Coast 1631; later the number was changed to 387-4511.

The two Risk girls greatly enjoyed the regular guests, especially children of similar ages. Among the long term guests who returned again and again that Karen and Sandra particularly remember were the Claytons from the Seattle area, with sons Steve, Tom, and Dick; the Ted Alverson family from California, with their children Denise, Carolyn, and David; the Bittermans who always stayed three

Cama Beach Resort house and store, with 1940s cars. *(Stanwood Area Historical Society, 2002_57_085)*

Many families have album pages of photos from their times at the resort. These photos are from 1939. *(Courtesy Laura Strance Poston)*

weeks, including their children David and Kathy; the Fullertons from California; and Jimmy and Jeannie Smith with their daughter Margaret.

Of the guests interviewed for this book, Laura Strance Poston has the earliest memories of the resort from her family's summers there in the early 1940s. She thinks of Cama Beach as "a family place. There were other families in every cabin, and everyone got along."

She tells of the times when her family stayed in Bungalow H (now relocated to the location of former Bungalow B) for a month each summer from 1939 through 1944 or '45. The family from Edmonds, Washington, included daughter Laura, son William, their parents, and an older girl, Charlotte, who lived with their family and helped their mother. Laura recalls that in January or February her father would ask if they should send in their deposit for the bungalow, and the children would enthusiastically reply, "Yes! Yes!"

She remembers the drive to the resort as seeming to be long. The family would take bedding and clothing with them and would pull a trailer behind the car, carrying items such as the children's bicycles, inner tubes for playing in the water, and some firewood. They would typically stop in Stanwood to stock up on perishable food items.

Her father was a dentist, and he and his wife typically were at Cama Beach only on the weekends, staying at home during the weekdays while he continued his dental practice and she helped out elderly parents. So Monday through Friday, Charlotte supervised the two younger children as sort of a "camp counselor." No car was available unless a parent was there.

Laura Strance Poston remembers the cooking in the cabins as primitive, such as making toast by cooking the bread between metal pieces on the stove. They built fires in the bungalow's fireplace.

The managers, Mr. and Mrs. Risk, were "the bosses. They were nice about it, but they had strict rules. They were like an extended parental presence."

One year Charlotte met a young man, Fred Herman, at Cama Beach when he came to visit the family staying in the bungalow next door. The two married that

Fred Herman and son John, c. 1946
(Courtesy Laura Strance Poston)

Charlotte Herman and son John, c. 1946
(Courtesy Laura Strance Poston)

fall. On leave from the military during World War II, Fred took movies of the children and others at Cama Beach, as well as of the road trip from Seattle at a time when the main highway was two lanes and the bridge to Camano was a steel truss structure. When the war was over, Fred returned and saw his two year old son John for the first time. He, Charlotte, and John immediately went to Cama Beach to stay for a week. Fred Herman later had a career as an architect.

Laura Strance Poston remembers that in the summer of 1944, the Risks had a new baby girl, Karen. The Strance family stopped going to Cama Beach the next year. Since the children were older, Laura wanted to go to Girl Scout camp and her brother Bill wanted to go to a Boy Scout camp. Their parents told them to choose, and the scout camps won.

Countless other guests also have vivid memories of the resort. In a May 31, 1992, letter to Sandra Risk Worthington, Margaret Barbey of Marysville wrote:

> At this time of year, our thoughts turn to Cama Beach. Together with my in-laws, we spent time there for most of 30 summers. Our albums are full of pictures—the fire pit, the rec. hall, the store, the bulkhead . . . There is even a 26" by 30" framed picture in our living room of the front porches of the cabins. How very sad that those days are gone! We sincerely hope that should the state buy Cama, they will keep it simple and beautiful.

A 1999 newsletter of the Cama Beach Institute quotes former long time guest David Alverson:

> I can't even begin to say how much this place means to me. My parents went there in 1937 while dating in high school, as a vacation spot that my grandfather discovered. In 1954, they took us children . . . for a vacation! . . . I can still remember the square dances, bean bag toss, Chinese Checkers, rocking in all the chairs around the fire in the hall, and the traveling movies . . . and of course, the nightly campfire with the tall fishing stories from Mr. Smith and others . . . I also remember renting rowboats, and riding down the boathouse tracks to splash into the water, then dropping the string hook to see if we could catch a crab at low tide. It was the BEST!

In the 1970s Daryl and Joan Conrad, then of Olympia, brought their children Mark and Susan regularly to Cama Beach for a number of years. The Conrads introduced two other families, the Cooks and the Harpers, and the three couples with their children would rent side-by-side waterfront cabins.

Daryl Conrad says, "It's a special place for us. We had some very good times up there. It was a beautiful, safe place for children." He states that one reason for initially choosing the resort was, "We're not camping people. We never did tent stuff. But at Cama, we had a roof over our heads, and we were right on the beach." He mentions liking the old wood stoves and the ice boxes, as well as the quaint instructions on the cabin wall for the use of rationing cards at the store. "But we didn't enjoy running to the bathrooms in the middle of the night."

Barbara and Tom Cook of Olympia, who were introduced to Cama by the Conrads, went there a number of years with their two children, Rob and Melanie. Barbara Cook writes of their visits in the 1970s, "As we crossed onto the island the anticipation grew, and then we dropped through the forest and, like falling through a rabbit hole, landed at Cama Beach where the clock had apparently stopped about 1944."

Tom and Barbara Cook's daughter, Melanie Cook-Hartley, speaks of "looking back as an adult at the simplicity of it. As kids, we created so much fun there. We had an incredible amount of freedom to explore. We could be gone hours at a time, and our parents never worried."

Her mother writes that, since the Cama visits occurred after the family lived in Ohio and Hawaii, "It occurs to me that our kids learned to be 'Northwesterners' at Cama Beach. They learned to eat seafood that wasn't fish. They learned to swim in cold salt water and love it. They discovered the joy of stinky seaweed."

Barbara Cook sums up the experience: "The lasting impression that I have of Cama Beach is of the viewscape. That stretch of beach went on forever! And undeveloped evergreen forest as the backdrop. I will never forget that view, and how privileged I felt, even then, to be able to spend some time there. It was so emotionally comforting to me to be in a place that felt timeless, uplifting even."

Melanie Cook-Hartley, now a mother of two herself says, "I remember it as a completely worry-less time. We search for that for our own kids now. To try to foster that imaginative, creative play. We made up our own adventures and games. We always came up with things to do."

Judy Graham of Olympia went to the resort with her family, the Beemans, from around age ten to thirteen. She remembers how beautiful Cama Beach was, including how clearly the stars could be seen at night. One memory is that her brother, then around one year old, walked for the first time at Cama. Judy drove a boat for the first time there, when her father rented one of the resort's boats and let her run it. She especially remembers playing cards in the evening and sitting around the fire, making and eating s'mores.

Chapin Krafft, his friend and neighbor Garth Wilson, and their older brothers, all from Seattle, began going to Cama Beach as children in the late 1950s. Sometimes the boys were with Chapin's parents, and sometimes with Garth's, and the families typically stayed for a week or two each summer. The boys did a lot of fishing. He remembers also going there once at Thanksgiving, and also at Easter. When the four boys were older, the parents would rent a bungalow for themselves, and the kids would stay in a small cabin but would go to the bungalow for dinner.

Although Chapin and Garth didn't do anything truly bad, "We were somewhat mischievous," Krafft says, "and we'd end up in hot water with Mrs. Risk." She asked they keep away from the old, decrepit Buick touring car behind the boathouse, but it was a big draw. "She'd always appear whenever we were by it. We developed a fear of being in trouble." One time they jumped over the sea wall and hid. They looked up, and she was standing on the sea wall, and we thought, "Where'd she come from!"

One day, the two boys rowed across to Whidbey Island in one of the resort's rowboats. Returning, they realized the currents were taking them away from where they wanted to go. A fisherman with an outboard motorboat towed them in. "Mrs. Risk had spotted us with binoculars and could see the currents were changing. We were in hot water, missing all day."

Another time, the two tried to find weights to use in casting their fishing lines from the shore. "The Cama Beach store only had trolling gear, not any for casting. So we carved a mold and tried stoking the stove in the cabin high enough to melt lead split shot. It never worked, but we burned a lot of wood and came close to burning down the cabin."

Much later, he and Garth went to Cama and rented one of the "fishermen's cabins" with their girlfriends. One of the girls brought out candles to set the mood for a romantic dinner. Chapin and Garth said, "No— Mrs. Risk doesn't allow candles in the cabins."

The girls replied that they'd just close the curtains, so no one else would know. Chapin said, "Mrs. Risk is everywhere!" The candles were lit anyway, and they closed the curtains, though the window was slid open a bit.

From outside the cabin came Muriel Risk's voice: "Mr. Krafft—no candles!"

"I'll never forget the look on their faces, the way their mouths dropped," Krafft says of the two young women.

Later yet, Chapin and his wife Kate stayed with another couple, Mark and Molly Mercer, in Bungalow J, then at the far north end of the resort. It was the Fourth of July holiday, and they had brought fireworks. Although in many years fireworks could be set off in the fire pit, Muriel Risk said there would be no fireworks that year due to the high forest fire danger.

The Mercers had brought a little car top sailboat, so when it got dark the men rowed out into the channel to shoot off the fireworks from the boat. Chapin relates, "Suddenly, we saw Dodge headlights on the shore, so we rowed farther out. Meanwhile, Muriel Risk knocked at the cabin door, calling, 'Mr. Krafft!' The two women hid in the shower at first, but finally they came to the door. Both women were pregnant at the time, and Kate could feel her baby churning. 'No fireworks!'" said Muriel.

Grandparents of Bill Koss at Cama Beach, c. 1950: Alva Koss, cousin, and Minnie Koss. Much later, from 1996 to 2002, Bill Koss was in charge of planning the new state park.

Summer Activities

Boating. Guests paid close attention to the tide tables, which listed the times and water levels of the high and low tides each day. It was much easier to get boats in and out of the sound when the tide was higher, and clam digging was practical only when the tides were lower.

The resort rented both row boats and power boats. Karen and Sandra learned to row at an early age. The names of four of the powered boats honored the family members: "Cama Queen," "Cama King," "Cama Princess I" (Karen's boat), and "Cama Princess II" (Sandra's boat).

Former marine railway at Cama Beach. (Stanwood Area Historical Society, 2002_57_372)

The resort's boats were stored in the large boathouse after it was built around 1950. The boats were lowered into the water and retrieved via the marine railway. The cart carrying the boats on the rails was attached to a steel cable, which was controlled by a winch powered by a large electric motor.

When the wind and currents were strong, it could sometimes be a challenge for guests to maneuver the boat onto the cart to be pulled in. Sometimes the guests would leave their boats on the beach, and Karen or Sandra would later guide them onto the cart.

Laura Strance Poston says of her own time at the resort, "It was really important to keep a rowboat for the week." They would drop lines from the boat to catch fish, using clams they'd dug as bait. Fishing for flounders, "We could see the fish and watch them on the bottom." They were required to do the cleaning themselves of any fish they caught and wanted to eat. The Howays who rented a nearby cabin had

A busy boating day at Cama Beach. *(Stanwood Area Historical Society, 2002_57_312*

their own motorboat, and their son Jim was allowed to use it by himself. "He was a speed demon."

When the resort's boats were lowered out of the boathouse on the marine railway, "The tide had to be just right. We had to hold onto the long wood poles on the rickety trolley and push off with them." There was a kelp bed farther down the bay, and she remembers her dad fishing for cod, and getting lines tangled in the kelp.

Laura Strance Poston and Nancy Howay Berg,1940s. *(Courtesy Laura Strance Poston)*

In later years, some guests brought their own power boats and anchored them in the cove or else south of the boathouse, and they and their families used the craft for water skiing as well as fishing. Fishermen also sometimes brought their own outboard motors and kept them in the lockers at the boathouse.

Swimming. Despite the coldness of the Saratoga Passage water, the summer swim lessons were popular, with a couple of sessions each day taught by Alma Woods from Marysville for two to four weeks. School buses often brought kids for the lessons, and some people tried to reserve a cabin for the times when the lessons were being taught. Karen and Sandra learned to swim well at a young age, and Karen remembers keeping two swim suits in use during the season. Red Cross Junior Life Saving cards could be issued at age twelve and up for those successfully completing the appropriate courses, from beginners on up. Red Cross swimming badges and certificates were also awarded.

Laura Strance Poston learned to swim at Cama in the early 1940s. Some years the family built a raft of driftwood logs, nailing flat boards on the top. They also used a flat log as a kickboard. She remembers how clear the water was.

The swim raft anchored off shore was a meeting place for older kids, as the smaller children couldn't get out to it. Sometimes young people would try to show how deep they could dive, bringing back a piece of eel grass from the bottom as proof.

Children floated on air mattresses and inner tubes, including a big Greyhound bus tube that could hold three persons. The tubes were kept inflated by the air compressor by the resort's gas pump. After a session of swimming, people rinsed off with a hose at the little gas station.

Girls playing in front of bungalow, 1940s. Courtesy Laura Strance Poston

Playing on the Beach. Laura Strance Poston remembers from the early 1940s that each year upon arriving at Cama, the children would rush to the beach to see if their favorite logs were still there. She remembers "lots of wonderful driftwood logs, with nooks and crannies. We'd fight over who would get which. We could spend hours playing there." They played games among the logs, and would go along the beach, jumping from log to log. "We had limits on how far we could go along the beach on our own, before we had to ask permission to go farther." They tried drying starfish on the logs so they wouldn't stink and something might be made from them. They also dug clay out of a bank by the beach and tried to make objects from it.

After World War II began, she remembers watching Navy ships in the distance through binoculars. Sometimes the children would row out into the bay after the ships had passed to rock in the swells left by the wakes. There were also tug boats towing log booms, though they didn't come close to shore.

She recalls lots of driftwood bonfires, supervised by adults, with roasting hot dogs and marshmallows. She speaks of the clam bakes—digging clams, catching fish, building fires and roasting corn in the coals.

Melanie Cook-Hartley learned how to skip rocks at Cama and would have contests with her dad and brother. "Every year, I'd get better." Her mother says, "Though we used the grounds of the resort for play activities, the pebbly beach was the reason we were there."

Sandra Risk Worthington recalls that, living at the resort while growing up, she'd lie on her stomach on the warm rocks on the beach and sift through the fine gravel and sand looking for tiny shells, which she collected in small jars. "It would take a long time to fill a jar." As a young child she also liked turning over larger rocks and seeing all the tiny crabs scurry off. She sometimes hunted for agates, though they were harder to find. She still enjoys hunting for shells and agates when she visits Cama.

Chapin Krafft remembers that his friend Garth's father, Claude Wilson, also loved walking the beach to look for agates. Mr. Wilson taught the boys his technique of looking when the sun was low in the sky and the tide was out. "We turned into avid agate hunters, and we'd have contests."

Fishing and Other Water-Related Sports. Fishing was a popular activity at the resort, especially in the earlier decades of operation. Although salmon were the most sought after, it was also common to catch bullheads and sole. In cooperation with other island resorts, Cama

The Payne family from Texas. (*Stanwood Area Historical Society, 2002_57_336*)

Beach cosponsored salmon derbies, with prizes for the largest fish caught in a limited period of time.

The resort store rented fishing poles. In the earlier years, live herring obtained from Utsalady on the northern end of the island were sold as bait. Later, after the live bait was no longer available, fish kept in brine were sold for that purpose, and finally

A catch at Cama Beach Resort. (*Stanwood Area Historical Society, 2002_57_361*)

frozen bait was sold. At the west end of the boathouse was an area for cleaning the fish that were caught, as well as lockers for outboard motors. Scraps from the fish cleaning were thrown onto the beach for seagulls to eat.

Chapin Krafft recalls, "We did a lot of fishing." He mentions his friend's father renting a boat, rowing out, and fishing for cutthroats, and another guest casting for flounder at the north end when the tide was out.

Clam digging was popular at low tides. Shovels could be rented at the store for 35 cents. A family of four was allowed to dig 20 pounds of clams per day. As the resort was only open three months per year, the clam beds were always productive. Hand cranked meat grinders could be checked out from the store for grinding up clams for chowder or patties. Recipes making use of clams were included in the goldenrod colored folders, the brochures that were sent out annually.

Occasionally guests, but more often employees, would anchor crab pots (cage-like traps) out in the sound. Tom Cook speaks enthusiastically of catching crabs, cooking them, and then having crab salad and other dishes. Daughter Melanie Cook-Hartley has a vivid memory of one afternoon during a low tide when they noticed large crabs and numerous flounders in the shallow water. The children got into rubber rafts and discovered they could trap the crabs with oars, and grab them with their hands, though the flounders were trickier. Soon her father and Daryl Conrad got involved also. "It was one of the most delicious meals I ever had," she says, mentioning the fresh fried fish, as well as clams. "It was sunny and beautiful. We had a fire outdoors, and it was a perfect summer evening. We sat and watched the sun go down."

Other Outdoor Activities. Many guests sat on chairs or on the sea wall, conversing in front of their cabins. Casual activities for children and older folks alike included walking the beach to look for unusual rocks or other objects, and skipping rocks on the water. Kids would try to walk the length of the beach without touching the ground, jumping from log to log.

A picnic at the Fire Square, early1990s. Pictured, left to right: Sandra Worthington; Tom and Beth Johnston, caretakers (center background); Michael and Brian Hamalainen (center foreground); Karen Hamalainen and Asko Hamalainen (right background).

Badminton equipment and baseballs could be checked out at the store, as could horse shoes for adult games at the horse shoe pits. A tetherball pole was heavily used by young people. Guests checked out tennis rackets and balls for use on the concrete tennis court south of the Recreation Hall. Daryl Conrad re-

Recreation Hall and tennis courts, c. 1940. (*Courtesy Mark Van Vliet; Stanwood Area Historical Society*)

calls how, in later years, the tennis court's net became droopy, "so we all felt like good players. We had to really have an 'off' day to hit the net with the ball."

Smaller children liked having their own little play area, located inside the curve at the base of the main hill road and screened by lilac, snowberry, and wild rose bushes. The mini-park included a teeter totter, swing, and a sand box. As darkness fell, children played hide and seek behind the bushes and trees.

Teenagers also liked to meet and talk at the play area. "We felt comfortable there," Melanie Cook-Hartley recalls." She particularly enjoyed using the teeter totter with Susan Conrad. "We'd go up and down on it, chatting away. It had a good spring to it, and we could almost bounce off."

In the evenings, a bonfire would be built in the fire square, burning driftwood collected from the beach after storms over the past winter. The fire square was a social gathering spot for teenagers, a neutral place to meet if a young guest had a crush on another. Often those present would roast hot dogs or s'mores in the fire.

Chapin Krafft recalls how he and his friend Garth would chase each other along the top of the sea wall. "One night in the dark Garth jumped off and tripped on the horseshoe pit and landed on a stake. Luckily, he just got bruised on his side."

Karen Hamalainen remembers picking berries each summer—the tiny wild red huckleberries, the strawberries in the children's play area, and the light orange salmonberries. In late July there was the scent of wild roses.

In those simpler days, there were not nearly so many brands of sun screens available for protection against burning; the choice was likely to be between Sea 'n' Ski suntan lotion or a basic sun block ointment.

Although there was a trail through the woods to Cranberry Lake at the far eastern end of the Cama Beach property, guests rarely walked that far, preferring to stay near the saltwater. The boggy lake remained a quiet spot for birds and other wildlife, including beavers until they were eventually shot by intruders.

Laura Strance Poston says her activities and those of the other children were oriented toward the outdoors. "We hiked on the trails in the woods. We picked berries when they were ripe." They especially liked a trail with madrona trees behind the cabins, and coming to a spot with a lovely view of the bay.

The Store. Resort guests have vivid memories of the store, often mentioning the unique odor. Laura Strance Poston says of her time there in the 1940s, "Normally our dad, as a dentist, wouldn't allow pop. But occasionally we got to go to the store and buy it." She remembers the smell of the store, and the mail cubbies, and looking into the glass counters to see what was there. In later years, she'd write letters, or

The store interior. On the far wall are the pigeonholes for keeping each cabin's record card and key. *(Stanwood Area Historical Society, 20022_57_214)*

postcards from the store, and would check for arriving mail. "It was fun to be told to go to the store and get some particular item." Since the store wasn't fully stocked, though, the family would go into town once a week or so to shop.

Chapin Krafft says when they were older, he and his friend "would flip a coin to see who'd get newspapers at the store," as Mrs. Risk would often keep them there talking longer than they'd prefer.

Melanie Cook-Hartley says, "I have fond memories of the store. I can

Melanie Ford Bissey, Cama Conference Coordinator, with some of the old wall posters at the store. *(Photo by Jeff Larsen, courtesy Seattle Post-Intelligencer, February 20, 2003)*

almost smell it, musty and salty." The kids would get pocket change and go to buy ice cream. "I remember the old freezer with the lid, which we'd lift up to pick out the ice cream. Sometimes we just went into the store to look at things; it was shady and cool."

Sandra Risk Worthington recalls, "I liked being there because nearly everyone came in at least once a day. It was a very social spot."

Indoor Activities. The Recreation Hall was open evenings, and this was the venue for many of the guests' activities. Rocking chairs were grouped around the fireplace for relaxed conversation. Some guests sat at the tables and played card games.

Other games, such as throwing bean bags through holes and tossing rubber canning jar rings onto a dowel, were available at one end of the hall's large central room. A quieter activity was putting together puzzles. Chapin Krafft recalls that he and his friend Garth Wilson were "avid checker players and bean bag throwers."

Recreation Hall interior.

Lee Risk owned several of his own prints of 16 mm. movies, including those featuring Laurel & Hardy and Mickey Mouse, though most films were borrowed from the public library and from Seattle firms. The same films were shown year after year, and many guests liked the familiarity.

TONIGHT – RECREATION LODGE
8 P.M.
GAMES – MOVIES – Community SING

COME AND HAVE
A GOOD TIME!

MOVIES TONIGHT!
8 P.M. – (STANDARD TIME)
RECREATION LODGE
25 MINUTE FILM IN COLOR
ON LOGGING IN NORTHWEST
ENTITLED:–
"MIRACLE IN WOOD"

PLUS CARTOON

Movie Notices posted by Lee Risk.
(Collection Stanwood Area Historical
Society)

Muriel Risk ran children's games in the Recreation Hall. The games included "Drop the Handkerchief" and "Button, Button, Who Has the Button," with children in a circle and a button being passed out of sight from hand to hand. Children also liked "Dodge Ball," played with a foam ball. Mrs. Risk also led singing, a favorite being "She'll Be Comin' 'Round the Mountain."

Square dancing was popular for older children and adults. There was usually a shortage of men, so often girls had to take the male part. Sandra Risk Worthington remembers square dancing to records with Ed Durlacher as the caller of the Top Hands dance group. She recalls, "'Dig for the oyster, Dive for the Clam' was a favorite square dance at Cama. 'Texas Star' was more difficult to learn. We felt lucky if we did it right."

Seattle square dance clubs also came up to Cama Beach. Chapin Krafft recalls "the biggest occasion I saw there was a festive square dance event or competition in the Rec Hall."

Guests could check out ping pong paddles and balls for use in the Ping Pong Pen building (later converted by State Parks into a restroom building).

For those who preferred to remain inside their own cabins, especially in rainy weather, an old radio was available for rental at a minimal charge.

The only time Melanie Cook-Hartley remembers being bored at Cama Beach was when there were a couple of rainy days and they had to stay inside. "My mother made us listen to a recording of Jonathan Livingston Seagull. It was like being sick."

The Work in the Summer Season

In earlier years, several employees lived on the site during busy periods. Some workers and their families made a year round home at the resort. A boatman, whose job was handling the craft, usually lived with his family in his own "Boatman's House" conveniently located next to the south side of the boathouse.

Often a family of employees stayed for an extended period in Cabin 28 behind the store. In the 1960s a mother and son team of Lucille and Martin Johnson lived there. Lucille did work such as cleaning cabins and mending linens, and Martin handled deliveries, stacked wood, cleaned ashes from the stoves, and cleared brush. Karen and Sandra also remember two teenagers, John and Becky Painter, who lived at the resort with their mother Rachel and Vern McCormick for a long period.

Typical resort jobs for women employees included sweeping the cabins, washing dishes and counters, and changing linens. Men would reset the fires in the wood burning stoves and in the fireplaces in the bungalows, restock ice, move beds out from the wall for cleaning, mop floors, and pick up garbage. Hired men also cut the grass using hand mowers. Muriel Risk did a lot of raking, so the resort grounds generally looked well kept. In later years she cut grass with a riding lawn mower which William Worthington, the author's father, helped buy and maintain.

In the evenings Lee Risk often drove to Everett to pick up big 300 pound blocks of ice from Bell Ice Co., making as many as four to five trips per week. Using an ice pick, he broke up the blocks into smaller chunks which were stored in a big ice box behind the store and at the boathouse, then delivered to cabins that were occupied.

Using one of the large International trucks, Lee also regularly picked up garbage from the cans at each cabin.

Cama Beach Resort's car, 1940s.

The Risks obtained wholesale groceries for the resort's store from Everett. Trucks delivered soda pop, dairy products, and bakery items to the store, as well as gasoline for the gas pump.

The store was open at scheduled hours in the afternoons and evenings, and daughter Sandra, or sometimes Karen, would staff the sales counter. Sandra remembers frequently having "store duty," usually 12:30-2, 4:30-5:30, or 7-8 p.m. Each of the Risk daughters was allowed one soda pop, ice cream, or candy bar per day. They remember the sound of the pop truck coming down the hill road, bottles rattling, to make a delivery. The store was also a good social meeting place, so the work had its enjoyable aspects.

At around age 11 to 13 years, first Karen, and then younger sister Sandra, began cleaning the cabins. Cousins Linda and Julia Shumm also worked at cleaning cabins for a few summers, sleeping nights on the bunk beds in the play room addition on the north end of the house. By far the most cleaning work was on the weekends after guests left and before new guests arrived. Checkout time for guests who were leaving was 1 p.m. on Saturday, and check-in time for arriving guests was 7 p.m.

The women employees did the remainder of the cleaning, each carrying a wooden fruit box with supplies such as Ajax scouring powder, rags, soap, Pine Sol disinfectant, and a brush for toilets. The laundry room on the south end of the Recreation Hall building housed laundry tubs with hot water for cleaning. The men often carried the hot water in milk cans for cleaning, including mopping floors, in more remote locations.

On the north end of the Recreation Hall building was a linen room where sheets, pillow cases, and blankets were stored to be supplied to the guests who chose to rent bedding rather than bring their own. The wool blankets were U.S. Navy surplus, and mattress covers for the beds were blue or white denim. In later years, the owners washed much of the laundry at the Camano Plaza.

Frequently, especially in periods of high demand, it was necessary to check the level of the water in the big cylindrical wooden storage tanks on the hill above the resort buildings, making sure sufficient water from the spring was available when needed.

The gravity-fed water system required frequent maintenance to keep operational. Lee Risk would have to hike the thousands of feet along the extremely steep bank to the spring and ensure the filter in the little pool was kept unclogged. The long water pipe hugging the side of the cliff was also in danger of damage from landslides in rainy weather. Maintaining footing on the steep hillside was difficult, and some falls injured Mr. Risk's knees, resulting in major problems in later years.

The Off-Season Work

Since the resort usually operated only from May through September, most maintenance and other necessary work was done in the off season.

With a gasoline powered buzz saw, Lee Risk cut wood into the proper lengths for burning in the stoves. He then split the chunks with an axe and wedges and used a hatchet to fashion smaller pieces for kindling. Afterwards he threw the wood in the back of a truck for hauling and stacked a supply at each cabin.

He also graded the gravel roads, using a truck to pull a four-wheeled grader with a big slanting blade. Fresh gravel was obtained from the beach by backing a truck through the gate in the sea wall near its south end. Ditches along the roads and elsewhere had to be cleaned regularly. Karen remembers a section of the old wooden sea wall near the south end of the resort washing out and many men working to replace it while the tide was out.

The wood floors in the cabins were refinished in the off-season as needed using a black stain. Muriel loved planting colorful flowers in the window boxes, as well as maintaining the flower beds around the store, the house, the front row cabins, the bungalows, and the children's play area.

Sandra remembers clipping the sword ferns as one of her jobs in the spring. Her mother taught her to sew at an early age, and she and other women would patch bed sheets. She also remembers patching the net for the tennis court many times.

Driftwood picked up from the beach would be thrown over the sea wall, then collected periodically using a garden cart and taken to the fire square to be burned on summer evenings.

In the early 1950s, Lee Risk began building a concrete sea wall to replace the log bulkheads. Working over a number of years during the months when the resort was closed for the season, he and a couple of hired men built the new barrier. Planning the work for the hours when the tide was low enough so as not to interfere, they would mix the concrete and pour it into the forms for one section, then move on to the next.

The fact that there were no guests at the resort during the off-season meant time for some leisure activities for the family. The family sometimes went on long trips, including to the East Coast, the Caribbean, and later to Europe. They often befriended students from other countries and would later visit them in their home towns in Europe. Lee and Muriel Risk drove regularly to Seattle, where they often went out to dinner and then to the Seattle Symphony or the opera. They occasionally took their daughters along on these trips to the city until the girls moved away from home to attend the University of Washington.

Muriel and Lee were both voracious readers. Lee Risk would typically visit the public library on the trips to Seattle and come home with a stack of books and opera records.

The Resort Structures Change over the Years

The Resort Layout. As shown by earlier photographs, the layout of parts of Cama Beach changed over time. The most conspicuous changes:

• An early diagram for the resort shows the cabins in straight rows, rather than the curved rows following the shoreline as they were actually built.

• A fire break was later added in the center of each of the double rows of waterfront cabins by relocating a cabin from each row.

Layout of Cama Beach Resort, c. 1940. Although much has remained the same, some differences are obvious: The cabin rows are continuous without a firebreak. The boats are stored in the two long parallel buildings toward the right. The Recreation Hall has an extension on the south end that was later removed. The owners' residence has not yet been built. The Boatman's House appears larger and oriented parallel to the water.

• Before the boathouse was built around 1950, there were two long boat sheds, and a longer marine railway to bring the boats to and from those sheds.

• Before the 1950s, an addition to the south end of the recreation hall provided what is thought to have been a sleeping porch. This was later removed, possibly so it wouldn't encroach on the tennis court space.

• The deluxe cabins were originally identical to the other waterfront cabins. The bathrooms were added to the rear later, converting the cabins into the "deluxe" versions.

• The rock walls in the area between the store and the cabins and in the fire square area were built in the early 1950s by a Mr. Stores from Anacortes.

• A major improvement to the resort was the replacement of the wood bulkhead by the concrete sea wall built in stages over several winters in the early 1950s by Lee Risk with hired help. He was proud of the sea wall and of the way it held up to the battering of even the worst storms. During the last months of his life in 1994, he reminisced about the project, obviously aware that it would be a lasting monument to his dedicated labors.

The Cabin Fires. With so many wooden buildings heated by wood-burning stoves, fires were a continual danger. On a Fourth of July holiday around 1950, when the resort was filled with guests, the boatman's wife tried to start a fire in the wood stove using a flammable liquid, either kerosene or gasoline. The resulting flash of flame set the cabin on fire, also burning the woman slightly. The boatman had shotgun shells stored in the building, and Karen Hamalainen remembers the shells exploding as the fire raged.

In the mid-1950s, Cabins 29, 30, and 31, formerly in the location of the new Retreat Lodge, all burned to the ground on the same day. Fortunately, not many guests were around. Sandra Worthington has a vivid memory of the cabins burning when she was eight years old or so. As the various volunteer firefighting units arrived down the hill road, her job was to direct them to the site of the fire.

The Recreation Hall Fire. The fire with by far the most impact on the resort destroyed the Recreation Hall. One evening in 1977 at our home in Olympia, Sandra received a phone call from her mother that the Hall had caught fire, and that the volunteer firefighters were there. Karen and her husband received a similar phone call at their Seattle home. By the time we all arrived at Cama Beach, the building had burned to the ground. Guests were staying in some of the cabins, but most chose to leave the next morning. The cause of the blaze was later determined to be faulty electrical wiring.

The destruction of the Recreation Hall meant the loss of a major activity center for the resort, as well as of the toilet and shower facilities for the two rows of waterfront cabins. Also destroyed were the movie projector and the old motion picture reels that Lee Risk had often shown as entertainment to guests, and virtually all of the resort's bedding.

As will be discussed later, even in the 21st century, rebuilding the hall still remains an intriguing possibility.

The Resort in its Last Years

By the time they were in their late 70s, Muriel and Lee Risks' declining health made it difficult for them to run the resort. The decreasing income from cabin rentals also meant it was hard to hire satisfactory employees and to maintain the buildings and the aging water system. Daughter Karen Hamalainen and her husband Asko moved with their two young sons from Seattle to Cama Home at Camano City to be more readily available to help on a daily basis. Still, keeping the resort functioning was a major challenge, especially as the Hamalainens also had their own jobs and their children to raise.

A combination of factors had led to the inexorable closing of the other resorts on Camano Island. These causes included the decline of the numbers of salmon in Puget Sound; the growing popularity of recreational vehicles for self-contained camping; increasing numbers of people owning their own boats and outboard motors; low priced air travel to vacation destinations farther from home; convenient, fast travel for longer distances on the interstate highway system; and other options for using leisure time.

Another major factor was increasing land values and the accompanying rise in property taxes, especially for waterfront acreage. Subdividing resort properties and selling the lots became much more attractive than renting out cabins, the income from which had to cover the property taxes as well as operating expenses. At Cama Beach, Muriel Risk had succeeded in placing most of the acreage in a "forest land" tax category, resulting in a much lower assessed value for all the property except the waterfront area. This helped the family to continue the resort operations for a longer period.

Although many guests still loved the serenity of Cama Beach and the rustic nature of the experience, not all enjoyed cooking and heating water on a wood stove or having to walk through the dark to the toilets in the middle of the night. As with the other resorts, over the years the numbers of guests returning steadily declined.

At last, in the spring of 1989, with Mr. and Mrs. Risk clearly unable to adequately handle another summer of visitors, it was obvious to the family that the time had come to end the resort's 55 years of operations. Letters were sent to recent guests informing them that the resort had closed.

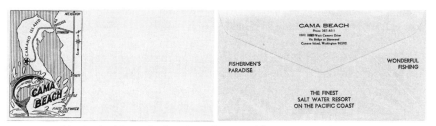

Front and back of goldenrod colored envelope used for Cama Beach Resort mailings.

PART FIVE

THE LONG PATH TO A STATE PARK

An Introduction to the Park Project Narrative

It was far from inevitable that Cama Beach would become a State Park. Those of us who strove toward that end encountered many obstacles—and many long delays. A number of times, the concept might well have died but for the persistence, and sometimes the rapid action, of key parties.

The construction of India's magnificent marble Taj Mahal took seventeen years. Getting Cama Beach State Park open to the public took a year more, even without completing two major new buildings. The family members involved throughout the project were middle-aged when it began; by the end, most people would probably see us as senior citizens. At least some of the many gray hairs accumulated by the time the park opened might reasonably be attributed to the frequent stresses of the process.

The Center for Wooden Boats (CWB) has been a partner in the project almost from the beginning. Dick Wagner, Founding Director of CWB and a true visionary, says of his own organization's remarkable success, "Nothing has been easy, nothing handed on a silver platter." The same is true of the opening of Cama Beach as a state park. People typically are astonished at the length of time involved, and they often ask, "How could it take so long?"

The following narrative is partly an effort toward answering that question. The park development was a large and complex undertaking. It challenged—and strained—the resources of a state agency with a relatively small staff to devote to any single project. The agency also encountered difficulties in dealing with a more extensive archaeological site than previously realized. Few people would be interested in every detail, but I've tried to give a feel for the more significant occurrences and the ups and downs, as the project progressed.

The section headings will help readers determine which parts of the narrative are of most interest to them personally. The text is based to a large extent on my own extensive notes of the meetings and phone calls that I, and often my wife Sandra, were involved in. I personally attended over two hundred park planning meetings, in addition to the uncounted lobbying contacts and thousands of hours of legal drafting, correspondence, and other paperwork. I've also made use of the many written materials I obtained from State Parks and Recreation Commission (State Parks) staff, consultants, and others over the years.

To help ensure that additional perspectives are included, I interviewed around thirty people who also had significant roles in planning and developing the park. Most were glad to talk of their participation. For those I wasn't able to interview, I nevertheless tried at least to touch on the aspects of the project in which they were involved.

Hundreds of additional meetings occurred internally in the State Parks agency, as well as among State Parks staff and the various consultants and other governmental agencies and tribal representatives.

A Note About the Project's Funding

The funding for the acquisition and development of Cama Beach as a state park had numerous twists and turns over the years, involving a complicated mix of donations of land and cash by the family; appropriations by the State Legislature; grants through various state and federal agencies; donations by individuals; grants from foundations; and eventually the sale of Certificates of Participation or COPS (bonds which must be repaid from revenues generated from cabin and room rentals and other income at the park itself). Although the family donations are substantial, ultimately the greater portion of the money came, in one form or another, from the taxpayers of the state. Sometimes, to the dismay of family members, parts of the project ended up costing far more than we'd ever envisioned.

In general, I decided not to get into actual dollar amounts in what follows as it is so difficult to succinctly summarize the many funding sources, the legislative appropriations, and the re-appropriations after delays. It is also mind-boggling to try to lay out the staging and the various components of the development work the money was spent on, but the information is available in public records for anyone having the skills and patience to analyze it.

The Earlier Concepts

As early as 1977, Cama Beach Resort's owners (the family) were thinking seriously about viable alternatives for operating the property. One possibility was continuing the resort operation, but by that time annual revenues had declined to amounts that were clearly far from sufficient to maintain the facility.

With over 400 acres of woods, the sale of timber obviously could bring in a significant amount of income. The family's younger generation—daughters Karen Risk Hamalainen and Sandra Risk Worthington, Karen's husband Asko, and myself (Sandra's husband)—selected a forestry management firm. With the consent of resort managers Muriel and Lee Risk, the firm designed and began to implement a sustainable timber production plan. The first commercial tree harvesting in many years was undertaken in 1978-79, on a selective basis with no clearcutting. However, disagreements arose between Muriel Risk and the foresters supervising the harvesting. She terminated the agreement with them, relying instead on the advice of the logging company owner. After a few months, the harvesting ended, the forestry plan lay mostly forgotten, and no further logging was done. However, a fairly considerable amount of funds had been generated to supplement income from the resort cabin rentals.

Although the family considered the logging to be a necessary short term solution, for the longer term they strongly preferred finding some way of continuing to make the obvious amenities of such a unique piece of property available to the public. Two possibilities discussed were those of a nonprofit nature center or a seminar/retreat center. However, both those options would require substantial funding to renovate the resort for year round use and to operate the facility. The fifty or so buildings were in various states of disrepair from deferred maintenance. Nearly all needed reroofing at a minimum, a huge task. The water system and sewage disposal systems were barely functional. The electrical wiring was outdated, as evidenced by the 1977 fire that burned down the Recreation Hall.

In the 1980s, a nonprofit organization based in Seattle founded by John and Collette Hoff, the Goodenough Community, showed interest in using the old resort for a retreat center. Representatives visited the property, and they held discussions with family members both there and in Seattle. The principals in the organization were enthusiastic about Cama Beach. Although there were subsequent meetings, and Sandra and I maintained contact with the group for several years, it became apparent to us that it was unlikely the organization had sufficient resources or skills to acquire and operate a facility as extensive as Cama.

We occasionally discussed approaching the state or the federal park systems, but Muriel Risk opposed turning her property into a public park. A strong believer in private property rights, she viewed nearby Camano Island State Park as competition for the resort to some degree. The overflow of visitors from the state park had also occasionally been a nuisance when they parked on Cama Beach land, and park visitors sometimes came onto the beach in front of the resort.

Another possibility was a donation of part or all of the land to a nature conservancy organization or other nonprofit, reserving a life estate in the older family members. This was an alternative later pursued at the same time as we were trying to work out plans with State Parks.

Over the years the family received many inquiries about possible development options, none of which we deemed suitable. Around 1990, an Everett attorney, Alan Donaldson, proposed a golf course and upscale resort on behalf of some Japanese investor clients. We explained why we felt it wasn't appropriate to clear most of the forest and put in a water and chemical-intensive facility for the benefit of relatively few users. He then came up with another privately funded proposal that was more acceptable in terms of the environmental stewardship and availability to the public, but the financial return to the family would have been far too low compared to the obvious value of the property.

In a 1990 letter to his daughter Sandra, Lee Risk suggested selling certain portions of the property to generate income to preserve and improve the main resort portion. However, the other family members felt extremely strongly that the property should remain intact. Selling even a small part would be an option only if other approaches failed.

The Risk Daughters and their Husbands

Because the family's next generation was responsible for initiating and following through on turning Cama Beach into a state park, it seems appropriate to briefly say more about these participants. I was one of them; to avoid awkward wording, I refer to myself in the third person in the short biographical section on the next page.

Karen Risk Hamalainen. Muriel and Lee Risk's older daughter, Karen Stradley Risk was born in 1944, and Cama Beach was her home throughout her childhood. She attended schools in Stanwood and then went to the University of Washington, ultimately earning a masters degree in social work, with extensive graduate work in public health. At the UW, she met her future husband Asko Hamalainen, a graduate student in fisheries from Finland.

The two were married in the house at Cama Beach. After a couple years in Finland and several in Seattle, in 1983 they moved with their sons Michael and Brian to Cama Home at Camano City.

The primary reason for the move was convenience in helping Karen's aging parents with the details of everyday life, as well as with maintaining the resort, thus enabling Muriel and Lee to continue living on the site. With fisheries jobs scarce, Asko established a home improvement business on the island. Karen commuted for some years to a social worker job at Everett General Hospital. With two young children, it was an extremely challenging time for the couple.

After the efforts began to urge the state to acquire Cama Beach as a park,

Sandra Risk Worthington (left) and Karen Risk Hamalainen at Cama Beach.

Karen worked to encourage local residents to become involved, and she and Asko frequently showed the property to interested officials and members of the public. More details on those activities are in following sections.

For several years before the resort area was taken over by State Parks, she and Asko hired and supervised various watchpersons for the property. Asko helped slow much of the deterioration of the buildings and the water system at Cama Beach, including reroofing most of the old resort buildings, while Karen worked at cleaning out the cabins and preserving items of historical interest. Now divorced, they both live in Bellingham.

During the planning process for the state park, Karen Hamalainen was a strong advocate for ensuring the facilities would be affordable for people of all income levels; for preserving the historic structures, as well as the artifacts from the resort and the former Native American presence; for ensuring protection of the wildlife habitat qualities of the forest; and for accurately interpreting the natural environment as well as the history of the site.

Sandra Risk Worthington. Sandra Stradley Risk was born in 1947. Cama Beach was her home for her entire childhood. She graduated from Stanwood High School in 1965, then attended the University of Washington and earned her master's degree in English from San Diego State.

She and her future husband, Gary Worthington, who grew up in Stanwood, dated in high school and later at the University of Washington when Gary attended law school. They were married in the family house at Cama Beach. After Gary finished his service as a Navy legal officer, they made their home in Olympia, Washington, where he worked as a lawyer for the State House of Representatives, specializing in environmental law, including parks issues.

Sandra taught in a middle school for ten years, then moved to Olympia High School, where she taught World and American Literature and writing for eighteen years before retiring.

After a year with the Washington Environmental Council, Gary went into private law practice in Olympia. He eventually left active legal work to write two historical novels set in India. During that period, the couple adopted a son, Shaun.

Throughout the process of turning Cama Beach into a park they both found living in Olympia to be convenient for attending the numerous meetings at State Parks headquarters and for lobbying at the State Legislature. Gary's legislative, legal, and writing experiences were highly useful many times in helping move the park project forward. Sandra reduced her teaching load for four years to attend park-related meetings and help with the planning process.

Partly due to her teaching experiences, Sandra insisted that environmental education for children should be an important focus at the park. She and Gary also value their experiences at various retreat centers, and the Retreat Lodge concept originated with them.

The First Park-Related Meetings

Early on the morning of November 10, 1990, Muriel Risk died. The remaining family members then began to more seriously pursue alternatives for Cama Beach. Fortunately, the family agreed in all significant respects on what should ideally be done with the land.

Although we had long wanted to preserve the property intact, preferably for the benefit of the public as a whole, there were some major concerns. One of the most obvious was that with over a mile of saltwater beach frontage, the land was extremely valuable. This would mean a high purchase price if it were sold as a whole, automatically eliminating most nonprofit organizations and other potentially public-spirited buyers.

The saga of Cama Beach becoming a Washington state park specifically began on the afternoon of December 11, 1990. Sandra and I met at a table in the Olympia Timberland Library with Cleve Pinnix, then Deputy Director of State Parks and a long time friend. We spread out photos and maps of the resort property and discussed how the family hoped to be able to preserve the land for access by the public. Enthusiastic about what he saw, Cleve showed the information to others in the agency, including the then Commission Director, Jan Tveten.

At that time, we were still exploring other options. In early 1991, I showed the photos and maps of Cama Beach to the representative of a major national land conservation organization and asked if it might be interested in working with us on preserving the land for the public good. The representative showed obvious condescension at my bothering him with what he considered an inappropriate property and said that the organization would only be interested if there were rare or endangered plants or animals to be protected. I couldn't demonstrate that this was the case, so the conversation was short.

Fortunately, other persons we approached were both much more interested and more pleasant to deal with. In February 1991, having read that representatives of various conservation organizations would be present, I went to an event near our home celebrating the acquisition of Grass Lake by the City of Olympia. Craig Lee, Regional Manager of The Trust for Public Land (TPL) was present, so I approached him with the same materials I'd shown to the other parties. He was immediately intrigued by the possibility of TPL helping acquire Cama Beach for public use. Typically, TPL would buy a property or acquire an option to purchase, and then it would hold the land until an appropriate governmental agency could obtain the funding to acquire title for the public. Lee toured the property with us that summer, and over a period of the next year or so, we continued to have discussions regarding that possibility.

Various key management and other staff persons from the State Parks soon visited Cama Beach for a preliminary evaluation of whether the site would be appropriate for a park, beginning with planner Jim Ellis in May 1991. First impressions are important in acquiring property as well as in meeting people, and Cama clearly made a positive impact upon the State Parks staff.

Ellis recalls Cleve Pinnix asking him to take a look at the property, and to keep an open mind, not being influenced by the fact that Pinnix knew Sandra and me well. Touring the resort for the first time with family members, he was immediately struck by the fact that "with a mile of shoreline, there was no other development in sight in both directions, and none in sight from anywhere on the 434 acres." Ellis met Lee Risk in the house on that visit, and he recalls, "Mr. Risk was emphatic about the property remaining together." Ellis particularly remembers the pictures on the wall in the store, as well as going into the boathouse and seeing the cog machinery for the marine railway.

He especially recalls hiking with family members through the forest to Cranberry Lake. The trail to the lake was then overgrown and not readily apparent. Our party split up, and he and Karen Hamalainen found themselves forcing their way through some high nettles and stumbling over rough, logged-over land outside the south boundary of the property. But in the end we all arrived at the lake with its twelve or so acres of quiet waters.

Additional visits by State Parks management and staff soon followed. Terry Doran, State Parks Northwest Region Manager throughout the Cama Beach project, says, "The first dramatic entrance to the beach site still sticks with me. It was very impressive."

When Dick Fankhauser, Chief of Site Planning and Acquisitions, was growing up, he regularly visited Ed Siers' Resort at Mission Beach on Tulalip Bay with his family. On his first trip to Cama Beach the old "kicker boats" in the boathouse reminded him of fishing in the bay with similar craft. He was especially impressed that the store and the gas pumps and cabins were just like what he remembered from his own resort visits in the 1950s and 60s.

Cleve Pinnix especially remembers going into the store on his first visit and seeing Karen Hamalainen pop open a bottle of decades-old soda. He also speaks of going into the boathouse and being impressed by the multitude of boats.

Regarding the property in general, Pinnix now says, "It's the kind of place that turns people into advocates. The land itself made friends."

But he recalls thinking initially that the site would be "enormously expensive." He remembers "wondering if the agency could pull it off, as it might mean no more acquisitions for years."

In June of 1991, on behalf of the family, I wrote an "Owners' Guidelines for Public Use of Cama Beach," which outlined our preferences concerning the form that any future park development should take. The statement read in part, "Any decision by the current owners to sell the property will be strongly influenced by the extent to which the following concepts are likely to be incorporated into the park." The list including, among others:

1990-91   Park Progress Timeline   (2008 Opening)

- All park development should be environmentally sound.
- The greater part of the forest cover and wildlife habitat should be retained as a natural preserve.
- Buildings should be energy efficient and appropriately designed for the setting.
- Recycling of garbage and other wastes should be practiced and taught to the maximum extent practicable.
- The park area should be a quiet, peaceful place for reflection and appreciating the natural environment.
- Facilities should be developed for an environmental learning center for stays of several days or longer.
- Motor vehicle access should be limited to those actually making use of the facilities (no drive-through sightseeing).
- General noise limits and restrictions on disruptive activities should be enforced.
- Some remnants of the historical use of the property as a resort should be retained.

At that time, we wanted to retain small portions of the waterfront area for future use by our own family members. We later dropped the idea, partly because of the awkwardness of private inholdings within public parks. We decided that if we wanted to stay at Cama, it was simpler for the agency, and also for us, if we were to rent overnight accommodations and make use of the property in the same way as other members of the public.

Dick Fankhauser recalls some resistance among a few State Parks commissioners and staff initially to acquiring Cama, in that "they didn't want to get a piece of property and be told what to do with it." Terry Doran remembers that though most of the State Parks staff were excited by the possibilities, there also were "some naysayers early on—it can't be done, or the agency would lose money on it."

Larry Fairleigh, who was involved at the headquarters management level throughout the entire project, most of the period as Assistant Director for Resource Development, says that many of the long time agency staffers were accustomed to thinking of a standard model for a new state park project. The usual state park included parking, a day use picnic area, restrooms, and generally a campground. And in those days, Fairleigh pointed out, when the state's population was much lower and housing developments were typically far away, there was little concern for surrounding a park with enough land to provide any kind of a buffer. So it was difficult for some staffers in the agency to grasp the idea of taking on a project that was both different and much larger than most.

But for the enthusiastic majority, Terry Doran remembers that the early thinking, which continues to be implemented, was that "Cama Beach would complement Camano Island State Park (which offers a large campground, picnic areas, and a public boat launch), not duplicate it."

Planner Jim Ellis also recalls that around this time there were discussions by the Commission about the need for State Parks to offer more options for overnight accommodations than the traditional campsites. With its many cabins, "Cama Beach fit right in."

On July 12, 1991, the family went for the first time before the entire panel of the State Parks and Recreation Commission, at the Commission's regular meeting in Anacortes. In addition to the family, numerous Camano and Stanwood area citizens attended and testified in support of the park. Also speaking in favor were Democratic State Senator Mary Margaret Haugen, who would become the Legislature's foremost advocate for the park, and Stanwood Mayor Robert Larson, who presented a letter of support from the Stanwood Chamber of Commerce and a resolution of the Stanwood City Council in support.

Mary Margaret Haugen knew the Risk family well, having grown up on Camano Island, gone to school in Stanwood, and ridden the school bus daily with the two Risk daughters. She, Muriel Risk and the daughters, and my own family also attended the same Stanwood church. She recalls that at the beginning of the park process, "Sandra and Karen came, and said they wanted to make Cama Beach into a state park. There was no question about it for me. I remember making a call to the director and being told the agency didn't want to get it, as they didn't have the funds. I told him to come and look at it before deciding that. And I said, 'I'll get you the money.'"

Haugen also represents Whidbey Island as part of her legislative district, and she observed that Whidbey already had so many good state parks, including South Whidbey, Fort Casey, Fort Ebey, Joseph Whidbey, and Deception Pass. "Camano also needed something special."

Bob Petersen of Long Beach had been recently appointed to the Commission and was attending his second meeting at the time. Afterwards, he and another newly appointed commissioner, Bruce Hilyer of Seattle, a private aircraft pilot, spent a week flying around the state, viewing the various park sites, including Cama.

Petersen had been building and designing wooden boats since he was a teenager. He had long been acquainted with Dick Wagner, the founding director of The Center for Wooden Boats (CWB) and was a CWB member himself. On August 9, 1991, he picked up Wagner at the CWB campus on Lake Union in Seattle, and they drove to Cama Beach. Petersen says they were "blown away by it, even though the day was dark and rainy." He remembers going into the boathouse for the first time. The roof was leaking and it was difficult to see inside, but it was also thrilling, "Like being explorers in King Tut's tomb." He remembers thinking that Cama would be an excellent site for expanding CWB's operations, and they were excitedly mentioning possibilities such as boat building classes and restoring the marine railway. Years later, Petersen says, "It developed way beyond what we dreamed of then."

Dick Wagner remembers Karen Hamalainen showing them around the resort on that visit, and that they looked at all the cabins and other buildings first. "It was a big surprise. I'd sailed past dozens of times, but had never seen any people there. From the water it had looked like an abandoned little village." He'd also had no idea what was in the boathouse, and when they went in, it was dark, and it took time for his eyes to adjust. Then he realized, "The whole floor was covered with boats, wall to wall!"

He says he then understood what the facility meant: "It was a capsule of history, of 1930s waterfront recreation." He remembers thinking at the time, though, that Cama Beach was too far away from Seattle for The Center for Wooden Boats to be involved with it. Plus, Camano Island had a smaller population then, and the property "was surrounded by boondocks," which meant CWB would likely not be able to have a large enough base of volunteers or financial supporters to sustain an operation.

But State Parks Commissioner Petersen had asked Wagner to give a written report to the Commission on the site's suitability for waterfront activities. In an August 12, 1991, letter to Petersen, Wagner wrote, "I would guess there is no other such 'living museum' in an accessible location. Go for it!"

However, there was not yet a firm commitment from State Parks or any other organization or public agency to pursue acquiring Cama Beach. In August 1991, on behalf of the family, I updated a draft of an "Invitation for Proposals Regarding Cama Beach Development." The paper was intended to solicit a creative plan from private parties with the necessary resources to turn the property into a viable undertaking. In addition to stating that "any development should be environmentally sound," the document said that "the property is ideal for such uses as a retreat center, conference center, environmental learning center/nature preserve, or a combination." We also asserted that "any development should not cater only to the wealthy."

Throughout 1991 we had numerous meetings with parks planner Jim Ellis, sometimes with other staff involved. In December 1991, Cleve Pinnix took over as Director of State Parks. He would continue in that position throughout the greater part of the Cama Beach park project process until retiring in late 2002.

We were still exploring alternatives with other public agencies, also. In September 1991, Joe Potter, NW Region Conservation Area Planner for the state Department of Natural Resources (DNR) toured the land. His report to the agency stated that the undeveloped portion of the property was a good candidate to be acquired for DNR's Natural Resources Conservation Area program. The developed resort area, however, was beyond the scope of any DNR program and so would best be managed by some agency other than DNR.

In May 1992 the proposal for the State Parks and Recreation Commission's 1993-95 Capital Budget/Ten Year Plan Request included amounts for "Acquisition,

Cama Beach, phase 1" and another sum for "phase 2" acquisition. But the project was only one among many on a long list.

Karen Hamalainen arranged for pieces in various local newspapers alerting interested members of the public that it was a good time to show support for Cama Beach becoming a park. She was quoted in the *North Snohomish News* as pointing out, "We're at a critical time. There are many projects competing for limited funds." Lee Risk said in a May 21, 1992, letter to daughter Sandra, "With *more* people than ever before alerted to the great potential of Cama Beach becoming a super-fine state park, the Washington Parks and Recreation Commission should feel, *increasingly*, the wishes of many citizens" (his emphasis).

A State Parks staff recommendation to pursue acquisition of Cama Beach was before the Commission at its June 1992 meeting in Bremerton. Testifying in support were Island County Commissioner Dwain Colby and our family. Senator Haugen was unable to attend, but she sent her son to testify. The Commission voted to authorize the staff to continue working toward obtaining the property.

In June 1992, a representative of the state Department of Natural Resources informed us that because State Parks was going to try to purchase the property, and because both agencies would apply for the funds through the IAC (Interagency Committee for Outdoor Recreation; now the Recreation and Conservation Office), DNR did not want to compete with State Parks for the same money and would not pursue the acquisition.

Although this meant one option for public ownership was eliminated, we were still hopeful of eventual success with State Parks. But until sufficient funds were actually made available through legislative appropriations, the park could not become a reality.

The Center for Wooden Boats Makes a Commitment to Cama

Founded in 1976, The Center for Wooden Boats has acquired an excellent reputation as a small craft museum with a growing collection of historic wooden boats at its facility on south Lake Union in Seattle. It also offers highly regarded hands-on courses for both adults and young people in subjects such as boat building, sailing, and maritime history. But by 1991 it was running out of room. The growing rental fleet needed frequent maintenance, and the boat shop was being used not only for that type of restoration, but for boat building classes and other instruction. More space was needed for the growing collection of historic boats, only a few of which could be exhibited at any one time.

The CWB board had asked Director Dick Wagner to look at additional sites beyond Lake Union. Wagner felt the sites should be in areas of sufficient population density, and although intrigued by Cama Beach after his first visit, he initially decided Camano Island did not qualify. At an all day board meeting, Wagner gave slide presentations of three possible sites he had identified: on Mercer Island, on Bainbridge Island, and on the Foss Waterway in Tacoma. He also "threw in some photos of Cama Beach, saved to the last." He'd felt the site was "attractive and of historical significance, but too far away." And with the relatively low population, it did not lend itself to people dropping by on impulse.

Wagner recalls, "Everyone was getting sleepy after lunch. But when they saw the Cama Beach photos, they all woke up, extremely excited, and insisted we contact the owners. They demanded a retreat there." Wagner contacted Karen Hamalainen, who agreed to an overnight stay, and around thirteen board members went to Cama on a Saturday. He says, "Even before dark, they thought it was really great, and said, 'Do what you have to do.'"

The CWB board, including then-chairman Carter Kerr, asked Wagner to do a survey of the membership to poll them about the possible second campus at Cama. He did so in a mailing with around four questions, accompanied by some photos. Wagner says around 99% responded favorably toward adding a facility at Cama Beach. CWB then developed a business plan which seemed financially feasible.

He remembers that there were a number of conversations with the family before and during this time. Sandra and I visited CWB's Seattle facility twice in that period and were greatly impressed with the potential for its programs at Cama Beach.

In 1993 and 1994, after consultations with Wayne McLaughlin, then State Parks concessions manager, I negotiated an "Interim Use Agreement" between the family and CWB for the boathouse area and three adjacent buildings, drafted with the expectation that the lease could eventually be taken over by State Parks. CWB member Steve Osborn and his wife Adrian moved into the boatman's house as on-site caretakers/managers for CWB. In late 1995, the family funded reroofing and repairs on the CWB buildings and also paid for CWB's hiring of Marty Gregory as site coordinator to supervise those repairs.

Since that time, CWB has actively collaborated with State Parks and others in the planning process for Cama Beach and advocated funding for the park from the State Legislature. CWB was initially designated by State Parks as an "anchor program" for Cama Beach, and later as an "enduring partner."

Formation of FOCIP; Public Support for the Park

An October 1992 piece in the *Skagit Valley Herald* had the headline, "Family wants to sell Camano Island property—but not to just anybody." Karen Hamalainen was active in contacting local community people about the need for public support for the state park project.

Of the pressures on her and her family at the time, she says, "It was a balancing act, being there whenever people came to show them the property and present it well, while at the same time being parents to young, challenging kids and helping out Dad so he could keep living on the site."

In March of 1993, the Friends of Cama (later renamed the Friends of Camano Island Parks, or "FOCIP") was formally established as a nonprofit corporation, with Carol Triplett and Beth Johnston, one of the interim caretakers at Cama, listed as the incorporators and as directors. The other directors listed on the Articles of Incorporation were Dodie Markey, Roy Hobbs, and Pam Pritzl.

Carol Triplett, who would eventually be the chair or co-chair of the organization throughout most of the period of the Cama Beach project, related her reasons for getting involved at that time. She and her husband Gwyn had moved to Camano Island a number of years before, made it their home, and recently retired. They had taken a trail building course, and although they had visited a lot of parks, they preferred to focus their efforts on Camano. They visited Cama and saw that it was "unique with all the cabins," and they were also inspired by a visit to Cranberry Lake. They saw Cama Beach as "huge and unique, and envisioned trails there, as well as reenacting the resort and offering environmental programs."

FOCIP volunteer Gwyn Triplett mowing at Cama Beach in 1990s. *(Courtesy Carol Triplett, Friends of Camano Island Parks)*

The Friends of Cama printed a brochure put together mainly by Carol Triplett headed, "HELP SAVE HISTORICAL CAMA BEACH, For a Future State Park." The main thrusts of the text were the need for generating additional interest and funding from the community, and the need to "convince the 1993 Legislature to commit money for the immediate purchase of this property." Meetings were held in May, including one attended by representatives of Washington Water Trails, primarily a kayaking organization, volunteers from The Center for Wooden Boats, and the Cama Beach owners. Numerous details were discussed regarding how to go about acquiring the property for the public and planning volunteer work on the site.

Carol Triplett and Sam Taniguchi at FOCIP work Party at Cama Beach, 1990s. *(Courtesy Carol Triplett, Friends of Camano Island Parks.*

An address list for FOC members around this time shows 73 names, most from Camano, but a few from other places in the Puget Sound region and one from California. The organization's volunteers often gathered for work parties to help maintain the grounds around the resort area.

In May 1993 a letter went out on the letterhead the Camano Island Homeowners Association (C.I.H.A.) asking that recipients write a letter to each of the State Parks commissioners asking each of them to support the acquisition of Cama Beach for a state park. The letter was signed by Jane C. Foltz, both as a Friend of Cama and as President of C.I.H.A.

Carol Triplett recalls that the Friends of Cama had a booth at the Mayfest festival and "pages and pages of people signing a petition to buy the park." A photo appeared in the *Stanwood/Camano News* of several local high school students who helped gather signatures and who planned to present them to the State Parks Commission.

State Representatives Sue Karahalios and Barry Sehlin of Oak Harbor also became early supporters. As the lead Republican on the House budget committee, Sehlin was to prove a key figure in future Cama funding efforts during a number of legislative sessions.

Stanwood students help Cama Beach

Stanwood High School students Dorothy Galbreath, Monica Pannek, Kelly Pranghofer, Doug Flickner, Kathy Eaton and James Daniels, left to right, put together petitions supporting the addition of Cama Beach on Camano Island to the state parks system. They plan to attend the state Parks and Recreation Commission meeting June 5 when Cama Beach's future as a state park is considered.

Students helping with petitions urging state to acquire Cama Beach for a park. *(Undated clipping from* Stanwood/Camano NEWS*)*

In Olympia, Ralph Munro, the popular and highly regarded Republican Secretary of State, was also an early and enthusiastic advocate for the park. He would voice his support at various times over the ensuing years.

Possible Methods of Funding

There were two main possibilities for obtaining state funding for the land purchases. A relatively new alternative was the Washington Wildlife and Recreation Program (WWRP). The Legislature had set up a competitive funding procedure for state and local parks and recreation projects, with the process administered by what was then the Interagency Committee for Outdoor Recreation (IAC). Various categories of projects had been established, and the most likely ones for which Cama Beach was qualified were the "State Parks" category and the "Water Access" category. Parks Planner Jim Ellis would present the supporting information for the Cama Beach project to an IAC panel, which would then use a scoring system to prioritize the projects competing in that category.

The funding would still depend on park advocates convincing the Legislature to appropriate sufficient money for the WWRP to fund the projects down through Cama Beach on the particular category's priority list.

If the WWRP process failed to provide enough money to include Cama, the other possible route for acquisition funds was a specific "line item" appropriation for Cama Beach in the state's capital budget. This would typically require an influential legislator to act as a "champion" for the project and convince the chair of the capital budget committee in either the House or the Senate to insert the funding. The legislative proponents would then have to ensure that the item remained in the budget until final approval by both houses, despite competition for the limited available funds by other projects.

The 1993 Legislature

Then-Director Cleve Pinnix says if Cama Beach had come along a few years earlier, there would likely have been no land acquisition money. The Washington Wildlife and Recreation Coalition, a statewide, nonpartisan organization made up of numerous organizations and individuals, lobbied the 1993 Legislature to appropriate substantial funds for the WWRP. Governor Lowry's proposed budget funded the program at $85 million, but by April near the end of the session, the program had been reduced in the Legislature to $50 million.

When the final budget was approved in May, after a major lobbying effort to restore the amount proposed by the Governor, the WWRP was funded at $65 million. But according to Larry Fairleigh, who was acting as capital budget coordinator for the State Parks Commission, this would not be enough to provide acquisition money for Cama Beach, as other state park projects were higher on the list.

During the legislative session Representative Barry Sehlin's office had received twenty to thirty phone calls in favor of acquiring Cama, with only one individual opposed due to concerns about increased traffic and possible vandalism. The 10th district legislators—Senator Haugen and Representatives Sehlin and Karahalios—decided to send a letter to State Parks asking that Cama Beach be given a higher priority for the funding. Others signing the letter included Representatives Hans Dunshee and Dave Quall, Congressman Jack Metcalf, and at least fifteen others.

It would still be up to the State Parks and Recreation Commission itself to decide if it wanted to shift funds from projects higher on the list and allocate them instead toward purchasing Cama. A major, two page spread in the *Stanwood/ Camano News* in May 1993 featured photos of the property. The lengthy article outlined the efforts of area citizens and legislators and the upcoming decision by the Commission.

A Major Hurdle: The Cost

On May 15, 1993, the family sent a formal letter to the State Parks and Recreation Commission, outlining the steps taken to date toward turning the property into a park, including efforts by the Friends of Cama, CWB, and other supporters, and stating that the family would be "glad to cooperate in working out whatever arrangements would make public ownership more feasible, including a phased acquisition." The letter reiterated, "We are still interested in donating a substantial portion of the sales proceeds toward development."

As yet, there had been no actual appraisal of the property. A tentative preliminary estimate was in the neighborhood of $15 to $17 million, more than most people had expected, even for such an obviously valuable piece of waterfront property.

On an evening in early June 1993, I received a disturbing phone call. Parks and Recreation commissioners were holding a meeting, and Tom France, then Assistant Director for Resources Development, wanted us to know that they had discussed the Cama Beach purchase. The commissioners would like to buy the property. But it was too expensive. The anticipated fair market value was more than the entire amount available for acquisitions state wide. The Commission couldn't see having that kind of money available for a single piece of property.

I hurriedly did some calculations, arriving at the concept of land donations by the family of around 60% of the total property value as matches for land purchases, spread over a number of phases. As extra incentives to encourage a speedy acquisition process, the first and last matching donations would be twice the value of the purchases. The land donations would be in addition to fairly substantial cash grants from the family for development work at the park. I showed the figures to my wife Sandra, who was busy, as she often was, reading and correcting her high school students' writing assignments. She quickly approved the idea, and I then phoned Karen Hamalainen, who immediately agreed with the proposal. I telephoned the agency with the outline of the concept, and we waited.

State Parks management reportedly was delighted with the idea. But the Commission still needed a firm offer in writing of what the family would be willing to accept for a purchase price. On June 11, 1993, I flew to Richland for a Commission meeting. On the plane was Joe Shorin, Assistant Attorney General assigned to State Parks, whom I met for the first time, and who later worked with me on drafting a number of park-related legal documents, as well as being involved in other aspects of the park project throughout its history. At the Commission meeting I presented a written "Proposal for Phased Acquisition Purchase of Cama Beach" by State Parks, at the core of which was the concept that the family would be donating land worth roughly $10,000,000, or approximately 60% of the total value of the entire property.

We would also donate back a significant portion of the purchase proceeds toward development of the property. The assumption was that the transactions would likely be spread out over as much as four biennia.

Those in the know say this document was a pivotal moment in ensuring that Cama Beach would become a state park. Then-Director Cleve Pinnix remembers thinking, "Oh my God, maybe there's a way to do this."

Commissioner Bob Petersen says, "The family made an offer that couldn't be refused. That turned the corner." He cites, as three significant factors, the family's willingness to space the acquisition by the state over a period of years, the offer of the land donations to go with the purchases, and the offer of further donations of cash for development.

Despite the importance of the moment, I do not remember any details about how Commission members reacted to the family's offer. Bob Petersen's recollection may help explain the Commission's lack of a memorable response at the time: he says the commissioners were "dumbfounded" because the offer was almost too much to absorb. "It was beyond what could have been expected," so everyone sat speechless, while the next item of business on the agenda was taken up.

The Commission did soon vote to begin acquiring Cama Beach, and the process of turning the former resort land into a state park was officially under way.

Over the ensuing months, the project received considerable regional press and television coverage. A June 29, 1993, article in *The Olympian* began, "An Olympia woman and her sister have agreed to a combined sale and donation of their family's beach resort on Camano Island so citizens can enjoy it as a state park." An editorial the following month was headed, "Sisters merit praise."

P-I/1992

Karen and Asko Hamalainen at Cama Beach, from a front page newspaper article headlined, "An island resort for the state: Sisters strike deal to turn their family property into park." *Seattle Post-Intelligencer, October 12, 1993.*

October 12, 1993, the *Seattle Post-Intelligencer* featured the project on the front page. The headline on an editorial the next day read, "Bargain park for the state." Also on October 13, Seattle's KOMO TV featured Cama Beach in its evening newscast.

An editorial in *The Seattle Times* on October 14 was titled, "Two generous sisters drive easy park bargain." And on November 1, 1993, Seattle's KING TV aired an *Evening Magazine* segment about Cama Beach.

Preliminary Planning Documents

The family had long been concerned about how to ensure that the development and operation of the future park would be aligned with the original concepts, particularly that the accommodations would remain affordable to all segments of the public, and that the natural and historic aspects of the site would be adequately protected as well as interpreted through appropriate educational programs. Restrictions to that effect in the deeds for the land donations and sales were not acceptable to the state.

In 1993, as an aid in planning, the family paid for an inventory and analysis of the site by Boykin Witherspoon III of Earth Use Research in Seattle. Witherspoon taught at the Department of Landscape Architecture at the University of Washington in Seattle, and partly as a result of his connections there, students under Professor Sally Shauman used Cama Beach as the focus of major class project. Four student groups each devised widely divergent concepts for developing the site into a park, and those plans were presented at a public meeting in a fire station on Camano Island in June 1993. No further direct use was made of the students' work. However, Witherspoon's final product regarding Cama Beach was a comb-bound booklet titled *Cama Beach Inventory and Analysis* with numerous maps depicting various resources of the site.

The Appraisal, and the First Land Transfers

A major step in State Parks' land acquisition process was to get a more precise figure for the worth of the property. Carlyle Staab, State Parks Lands Agent, ordered a full professional appraisal. The final appraiser's report in February 1994 arrived at a total value for the land and timber at $16.5 million. Even with the majority of the land value donated, it would be necessary to spread the state's purchases out over a number of biennia.

The first phase of land acquisition was in 1994, labeled "Phase 1A." I spent many hours at my own desk with maps of Cama Beach, an engineer's scale, and a calculator before meeting with parks planner Jim Ellis over the complex process of carving out appropriate pieces of property for (a) the purchased acquisition and (b) the family's matching donation of double the value of the purchased piece. Using formulas set out in the original appraisal report, we created boundary lines delineating parcels that were of the specific dollar values needed.

Legislators in one biennium cannot bind legislators in future biennia to provide specific appropriations. Consequently, there could be no absolute guarantee that more money would be available for future acquisitions, so the pieces to be transferred also had to be usable by themselves for State Park purposes, including having suitable means of access. And the land remaining in the family's ownership also had to be viable for alternative uses with appropriate access.

In this case, after outlining on a map what seemed to be reasonable parcels to transfer, Jim Ellis, parks engineer Joe Gustino, and I traveled to Cama Beach to look at the parcels to ensure they were suitable. The areas passed inspection. Ellis particularly remembers a highlight of that visit was "going down the ravine with the stream at the bottom, and seeing the eagle's nest."

The conclusion of the process was a sale to State Parks in June 1994 of 610 feet of waterfront at the far south end of the Cama Beach land, including the western portion of the stream and its ravine, and a matching donation of adjacent acreage. Since Cama Beach did not yet have its own staff, Howard Adams, the manager at nearby Camano Island State Park, would have charge of Cama, too. Ranger Roy Johnson, also at Camano, would assist him.

Cleve Pinnix says he found working out the details of the phased donations and purchases to be fascinating, including a later unprecedented step of hiring private outside legal counsel with particular expertise in structuring the various aspects. "It was a leap of faith on the part of the family as there was no assurance of future appropriations. There was a risk for both the agency and the family. There has been nothing before, or since, with that type of long term acquisition in pieces."

The Vision Statement

Around this time, a *Vision Statement* for the future park was jointly drafted with input from State Parks staff, the family, and other interested parties. Planner Jim Ellis feels the document was highly important: "It involved all the stakeholders at the beginning, and it put everyone on the same track with some fairly specific tenets in it."

The tenets included such concepts as "Development and operation of the park emphasizes stewardship of its land and water resources. Recycling of wastes is demonstrated and practiced. Development and operation of the park retain the character-defining features of the historic site . . . The park's outstanding educational qualities are available to individuals and groups of varied ages through development of educational and interpretive features, including an environmental learning and conference center and trails."

The *Vision Statement* continues to provide an overall philosophy for Cama Beach State Park, and the park design and operations have been measured against it. A copy of the final version is in Appendix 1.

1990-91   **1994**   Park Progress Timeline   (2008 Opening)

Beach Watchers

Another organization with major involvement at Cama Beach over the years is the Island County Beach Watchers. The group was started in 1989 by Don Meehan, Director of Washington State University Island County Extension. To become environmental educators, volunteers receive over a hundred hours of training by experts, including field trips to various shoreline sites. Karen Hamalainen was part of one of the first classes in 1990, driving with others from Camano Island to Coupeville for two days of classes each week for seven weeks.

Hamalainen invited Meehan to see Cama Beach. Meehan says, "The first visit was truly a step back in time. I fell in love with it immediately and realized how important it was to save it." Although as a university program WSU Extension would not normally get involved in legislative policy issues, Meehan added his voice to encourage public ownership of the property. He also participated in meetings such as one on Camano Island in 1996 to help organize a private nonprofit foundation that became the Cama Beach Institute.

Over the years, Cama's relatively pristine beach became a venue for Beach Watcher training and projects. One of the projects included a comprehensive reference notebook for future use by docents and others at the park covering topics such as the history, geology, marine life, and upland flora and fauna. State Parks also eventually asked Beach Watchers to collect data for use in applying for permits to rebuild the marine railway at Cama.

Importantly, it was envisioned that when the park opened to the public, Beach Watchers would provide volunteers to staff an office and to educate the public, especially about the marine environment.

Some Intervening Events and Concerns for the Family

In Lee Risk's final years, whenever he wasn't reading library books, he would lie on the sofa in the living room of the house at Cama Beach listening to opera records or watching televised football games of the University of Washington Huskies.

Gazing out the windows at the view of Saratoga Passage, he sometimes commented on how lucky he was to be able to spend his final years in such a beautiful setting. He died on May 12, 1994, at the age of 85, shortly before the first transfers to the state. He had made it clear that he was enthusiastic about the plans that would keep the property intact into the far future for the enjoyment of the public.

Throughout this period, Karen and Asko Hamalainen, who continued to live at nearby Cama Home, arranged for a continuing series of caretakers to live on the site to act as watchpersons. It was often challenging to find reliable and responsible individuals willing to move to Cama for minimal or no compensation except free housing or a waterfront site for a recreation vehicle.

Another challenge was keeping the aging, spring-fed water supply system functioning. Asko handled this chore as well as plumbing work at the resort in general. Occasionally a landslide would make repairs necessary on the water line that ran along the side of the bluff. The big, round, wooden water tanks in the woods above the resort buildings sometimes sprang leaks that needed to be patched. Too, the gates at the county road would occasionally be damaged by vandalism, and Asko would do the repairs.

Fresh water suitable for drinking is a limited resource, and this is especially true on Camano Island. In anticipation of the large amount of water that would be needed at the future park, in June 1994 I submitted an application to the State Department of Ecology for rights to withdraw ground water. The estimate of the quantity was based on information provided by Joe Gustino, State Parks engineer. It turned out to be fortunate that the application was submitted so early as the state Department of Ecology (DOE), which adjudicates water rights, was several years behind in its process. Ultimately, the rights were in fact approved by DOE before the actual need.

Taxation Difficulties. An additional problem for the family in the early years of the land transfers was a lack of cooperation by the Island County assessor in office at the time. Although the developed waterfront area was taxed at fair market value, the bulk of the Cama Beach acreage had been classified as forest land for property tax purposes. This resulted in a greatly reduced tax rate, making it feasible for the family to hold on to the parcels so the pieces could be deeded to the state at the appropriate time. Upon the first transfer of land to the state, despite the fact that the land would remain wooded, the assessor removed the entirety of the Cama Beach land from the forest tax category under the reasoning that the land was held for future park purposes, not for timber production. This resulted in a sudden, immense tax bill for the family. Assessors in other counties had taken a less strict approach in similar circumstances, since the land was being held for a future public purpose and was in fact retaining its forest cover. An appeal to the State Board of Tax Appeals only partly resolved the concern.

In the next legislative session, Senator Mary Margaret Haugen and Representative Barry Sehlin introduced bills in their respective houses to rectify the situation. The legislation passed and was signed into law by Governor Lowry. The assessor was forced to comply, but he continued to interpret even the amended law as strictly as possible, resulting in additional major difficulties for the family on a couple of occasions.

CWB Classes Offered for the First Time. In this same time period, The Center for Wooden Boats began holding limited short term classes at the boathouse at Cama Beach. In a course in the summer of 1994, nine Stanwood-Camano teens built a wood boat. The following year, in May 1995, a class offered by CWB included boat building for students from an alternative high school in the Seattle area, with the students staying in tents at Cama.

Asko Hamalainen and the Huge Roofing Project. By late 1992, it had become obvious that the historic resort buildings were likely to be preserved and used by the public. So Asko Hamalainen began the huge task of reroofing the buildings. Enthusiastic about the future of the property he cared so much about, he volunteered much of his time, sometimes with Paul Kallock or another person also working as hired help. He worked with CWB volunteers on the reroofing the Boathouse. Additional volunteers helped at times on the cabins, including among others a Kiwanis crew, Rotary Club members, and a Windermere Real Estate/Dan Garrison, Inc. crew. The family paid for the materials.

The project was frequently slowed when rotted boards on the edges of the roof would have to be replaced before new shingles could be put on. Hamalainen recalls the considerable effort he went to match the boards, as "the new lumber didn't fit with the old wood." He and volunteer helpers tore down 40' by 140' chicken coops at another site to obtain lumber that would be a better match. He also bought weathered boards, often with knot holes, from Oso Lumber "for thirty cents on the dollar." These were boards that no one else would have been likely to want, but which

Windermere Real Estate/Dan Garrison crew re-roofing Cama Beach cabin in June 1994. Volunteering were Jay Lien, Dan Lien, Jim Joyce, Bob Nelson, Ken Lee, Tom Wokasch, Dave Hedeen, Tom Lund, Steve Love, and Roger Nelson. *(Courtesy Dave Pinkham, Stanwood/Camano NEWS.)*

went well with the older wood at Cama. For areas that would be visible on the exterior, he also often moved boards from higher on a cabin roof down to the edges to better match the existing wood.

By the end of five years, all twenty-four of the small cabins, the Boathouse, the ping pong building, the shop, and all of the deluxe cabins except for half of Cabin 32 bore new roofs.

These roofs protected the structures from considerable further deterioration for a period of around fifteen years until 2007, when the buildings were at last fully rehabilitated. The old resort structures would have been in far worse shape, and much more challenging to renovate, had it not been for earlier reroofing project by Hamalainen and the other volunteers.

The 1995 Legislature; and the Second Land Transfers

Funds were tight in the 1995 legislative session, and the initial version of the budget in the state House of Representatives did not include money for another land purchase at Cama Beach. Sandra and I met with Senator Mary Margaret Haugen, who assured us she would work to secure the

Local Rotarian Scott Harris (foreground), and Gil Powell (right) and his son and daughter re-roofing a Cama Beach cabin. Seven Stanwood-Camano Rotary Club members volunteered on a Saturday in November, 1993. *(Courtesy Dave Pinkham, Stanwood/Camano NEWS)*

necessary appropriation. Senators Dan McDonald of Bellevue, Karen Fraser of Olympia, and Harriet Spanel of Bellingham were early supporters of the project. In the House, Representative Barry Sehlin of Oak Harbor also worked to secure funding for Cama. Mike Ryherd, an experienced lobbyist, volunteered his help.

The list of priorities for the Washington Wildlife and Recreation Program (WWRP) included the next phase at Cama Beach; the problem was getting the program funded at a sufficient level. Fortunately, Democratic Governor Mike Lowry was a strong proponent of parks and recreation, and he insisted on substantial park acquisition funds through that program. In final capital budget, the WWRP did include enough to fund half of the amount requested for Cama Beach.

The project was featured on the front page of the Snohomish County section of *The Seattle Times* on June 15, 1995. The headline read, "One family's gift to you: Park on Camano Island." A favorable editorial appeared the following Sunday.

I went through another process with State Parks staff to delineate appropriate parcels to transfer in what was termed "Phase 1 B." In July 1995 the family deeded Cranberry Lake and some intervening parcels west of the lake.

On August 31, 1995, Governor Lowry toured Cama Beach. In a brief speech to State Parks staff, volunteers, and the former owners on the waterfront, he said, "People will come here forever, asking, 'Who had the foresight to make this happen?' I want to thank everyone here, but mostly the family for its unselfish act."

At that time, two more phases of purchase still remained to be funded.

The Master Plan

A continuing concern for the family was ensuring that the park would be designed to incorporate the principles embodied in the *Vision Statement*. State Parks' Dick Fankhauser recommended development of a more detailed official "master plan" to provide

Governor Mike Lowry (center left) at Cama Beach with Parks Director Cleve Pinnix (center right), August 1995. On the right facing the camera are Gary Worthington and Asko Hamalainen. Governor Lowry strongly advocated more funding for parks and recreation lands.

specific, mutually acceptable guidelines. The process of developing the plan would provide opportunities for input from all interested parties, including State Parks staff, the family, interested user groups, the public in general.

But the agency did not have funds available to pay for such a plan. The family therefore agreed to hire independent consultants to conduct the process and develop the master plan. With feedback from Jim Ellis, I drafted detailed procedures for impartially selecting the best qualified consulting firm. The process was modeled on that used by the State of Washington's Department of General Administration, beginning with advertising for interested parties to first submit a Statement of Qualifications. On a specified date, representatives of the five prospective consultant teams all toured the site. In response to being provided with copies of the *Vision Statement*, one consultant expressed a wish to Jim Ellis that "every project would start out this way, with direction from day one."

Three finalists were selected from the applicants' submittals. During the month of April 1995, each of the three firms hosted family members and State Parks planner Jim Ellis on visits to their respective offices and to projects they had done previously. On April 28, at State Parks Puget Sound Region Headquarters in Auburn, each of the firms made formal presentations to a five person selection panel, including two State Parks staff members, two family representatives, and a staff person from the Interagency Committee for Outdoor Recreation. Each of the applicant teams was impressively qualified, and the results of a scoring process by the interview panel resulted in the equivalent of a tie. The final selection was therefore left to the family, and after extensive phone discussions, the Atelier team headed by Janis Snoey and David Ringstrom was hired.

Snoey says of her original impression of Cama Beach, "It brought tears to my eyes, walking down the hill and looking out over the resort, and thinking of the fact of the donation, and what the place meant." She says she and her firm were so eager to be selected, "We put more time and effort in to the Statement of Qualifications than on any other project."

An extensive planning process ensued, with numerous meetings including three workshops with interested parties at Cama Beach and a public meeting in February 1996 at the Terry's Corner Fire Station on Camano Island. Janis Snoey says, "It was really pleasurable working with the interested groups. It was exactly the type of work we became landscape architects to do." She saw her role, and the role of the others in her firm as "guiding," rather than as generating the master plan on their own.

State Parks Northwest Region Manager Terry Doran, who made a point to visit the park with the agency planners at critical stages throughout the project, recounts how "the spaces at Cama were critical and mean a lot. The goal was to enhance what's there, not change it."

A main feature of the plan was placing the parking areas on the higher elevations, to keep most of the vehicular traffic away from the waterfront area, thereby preserving the serenity of the site. How to handle access to the park for physically less able persons was therefore a major concern. The master plan included a 1,200 foot long "boardwalk" along the hillside, from the Retreat Lodge area to the Store area, providing a gently sloping ramp suitable for wheelchairs. This concept was eliminated several years later as being no longer required after the Dining Hall was moved up by the Retreat Lodge.

Larson Anthropological/Archaeological Services did a Cultural Resource Assessment, including an evaluation of the underlying archaeological middens. Contacts by Larson during the process included the Tulalip Tribes, the Swinomish Tribe, and the Snohomish Tribe. A well known expert, Robert Z. Melnick, was also involved in writing the historical/cultural resources portion of the plan.

The Miller/Hull Partnership of Seattle served as the architects for the master plan, including providing preliminary sketched designs for a Dining Hall and a Retreat Lodge. D'Amato Conversano Inc. were the structural engineers; geotechnical reports were by AGRA; and a traffic study was done by Transportation Solutions, Inc.

Part of the process included an Environmental Checklist for the *Master Plan* by Herrera Environmental Consultants and a Declaration of Non-significance (DNS) in compliance with the State Environmental Policy Act. The DNS embodied a formal determination, based on the information in the checklist, that the plan would result in no significant adverse consequences to the environment.

The *Cama Beach State Park Master Plan* was formally approved by the State Parks and Recreation Commission on January 24, 1997. For the most part, the future development of the park followed the concepts in the plan with some modifications to reflect additional or new information and changing circumstances.

Janis Snoey says she feels the end product of the planning process was wonderful: "Cama Beach was going to become what *it wanted* to be; it just needed a hand to guide it."

Funding Plans for Park Development. In May 1996 a meeting was held at the Northwest Region office in Burlington to determine the phasing of development work. Present were Terry Doran, Allison Alderman, Jim Ellis from State Parks, Janis Snoey and Dave Ringstrom from Atelier, and the four family members.

Funding for Cama has always been a complicated assembling of money from various sources, and at least nine sources were identified at this meeting, some definite, and some only possibilities for development money. Principal potential sources included COPs (state certificates of participation); 057 (the state's general construction account); I-215 (grants through the IAC from power boat taxes, especially for mooring buoys in this case); 108 for road work; ISTEA matching federal transportation grants; ALEA (Aquatic Land Enhancement Account) through the state Department of Natural Resources for water access development; and WWRP (Washington Wildlife and Recreation Program) grants that are competitive in different categories. A few days later, at a meeting with Director Pinnix and Planning Manager Bill Koss, the family pledged a substantial amount in cash toward the first phase of development.

Interim Events and Concerns

The Sea Wall. The condition of the sea wall was a continuing concern. In September 1996 a detailed evaluation of the wall was done by D'Amato Conversano Inc. (DCI), a Kirkland consulting engineering firm. The study concluded that the sea wall in general was in very good shape, but that there were some specific spots that should be given attention, including "armoring" the base of the wall south of the boathouse and at the wall's southern end with stones and filter fabric, sandbagging the two gates in the winter for additional support against storm surges, and filling some cracks in the wall with epoxy.

The Cama Oral History Project; the Cama Foundation (Later the Cama Beach Institute.) In late 1996 an oral history project was launched by Karen Hamalainen, with numerous interviews conducted mostly by Jessica Stone. Many elderly, life long residents of the Camano Island area were asked a standard series of questions, with their responses recorded on audio tapes. Some of the interviews were later transcribed and were sources for an earlier part of this book. The materials are now housed by the Stanwood Area Historical Society.

Several of the questions related specifically to the residents' experiences of Cama Beach. Ole Eide visited the site around 1923, and he remarks how bare the hill appeared due to the prior logging. Other questions dealt with earlier life in the

Camano/Stanwood area in general. Overall, the information compiled is a valuable source about several decades of local history.

Largely through efforts and funding by Karen Hamalainen, an initial meeting of The Cama Foundation Project was held in October 1996 at the Hamalainen home on Camano Island with Jessica Stone acting as interim facilitator. Followup meetings were held afterwards.

David Herrick was one of the early participants. A resident of Seattle, he had read a news account of the family donating land for a state park. He visited the site, and thought, "Wow, what a special place this is. I had never seen anything that had that type of character to it." Interested in land for a getaway, he soon bought property nearby which his family used first as a camping site and eventually as a house site. He saw a notice in the *Stanwood/Camano News* about an organizing meeting for a Cama Foundation, and as a Certified Public Accountant, he soon found himself the organization's treasurer, and he participated in park planning efforts over a number of ensuing years.

In 1998 the Cama Foundation's name was changed to the Cama Beach Institute (CBI). By that time, Linde DeVere, who had been hired as executive director, was working on a draft of an Operational Business Plan. Most of those involved assumed that State Parks would likely enter into a contract with CBI, which would operate the educational and environmental programs at Cama Beach, and which would also be taking the reservations for the overnight accommodations for people attending programs. CBI would get most of its operating funds from the state in exchange for initiating and conducting these functions.

In May 1999 a meeting was held between CBI and region State Parks administrators at which it was decided to draft an interim operating agreement describing the relationship between the two entities. As a public agency, State Parks could not show favoritism to a particular private group, so CBI would have to provide value to the state and be able to sustain itself.

David Herrick developed a pilot project for CBI in which oral and videotaped histories from persons with a prior contact with the property would be transcribed. CBI would establish an email and mail database of former users of the land. It would compile existing photos and would provide continuing newspaper publicity and rotating photos on a web site.

However, DeVere was finding it increasingly difficult to work with the agency in trying to offer some limited programs at the park. In early July, it was abruptly decided within the State Parks agency that the agency itself would operate the programs and handle reservations. There now appeared to be little role for CBI at the park. Without the anticipated funds from the state, CBI was in no financial position

to continue with a paid staff person, so the board felt it had little choice but to terminate Linde DeVere as executive director.

Although CBI continued to exist for some time with board member David Herrick doing much of the coordination, the organization's role became more advisory, providing citizen input on planning the park. Looking back, Herrick says, "It eventually became clear that CBI was just too early in the game. It was too theoretical trying to implement programs. The park opening was so far off, and it kept getting pushed back and back and back, so it became less real."

The Third Phase of Land Transfers

Transfers for the third phase of four land purchases and donations (somewhat confusingly labeled "Phase 2") were made in March 1997. This phase included the flat beachfront with the resort buildings.

Due to federal income tax laws providing a five year limit for deducting a charitable contribution, the agency and the family agreed that it was appropriate to delay some land donations into the future. After consultations with a Seattle law firm with expertise in the area, State Parks and the family signed an agreement with a schedule providing for donating a specified parcel every five years. The family granted the state the right to use those parcels prior to the donations and to manage them as if they were in fact part of the park.

IAC Rankings; The 1997 Legislative Session

Jim Ellis recalls making the presentations for Cama Beach funding to the IAC as part of the WWRP prioritizing process: "The whole package was not typical. The *Vision Statement*, the Master Plan, the donations from the family, all worked in the project's favor." Plus, "People had stayed in old fishing resorts, and they were intrigued by the lore and culture."

In August 1996, the IAC came out with its ranked list of statewide projects. Supporters were relieved that the fourth, and final, phase of Cama Beach acquisition was listed as the number one priority in the State Parks category, and as number two for the Water Access category. This almost assured the money would become available, assuming any reasonable legislative appropriation.

However, in the 1997 legislative session the capital funding was in question for much of the time, as were operating funds requested to hire the park's staff. Cama supporters coordinated with Rex Derr, the agency's legislative liaison at the time (and now its Director) to keep abreast of the situation. Both the House and the Senate were Republican-controlled, and Governor Gary Locke had begun his first term.

Fortunately, there was key bipartisan support for funding parks in general and Cama Beach in particular. Senate Majority Leader Dan McDonald, who was enthusiastic about Cama Beach as a result of earlier times on Camano Island, was an influential voice for the park. Senator Haugen and Representative Sehlin were again crucial in including Cama Beach funding, and Representative Dave Anderson of Whidbey Island also helped.

Supporters were relieved at the end of April when sufficient funds were at last authorized for the final phase of land purchases. Capital funds were also included for the upland parking lots, entrance road, and utilities; and authorization was granted for selling Certificate of Participation (COP) bonds to build a major new lodge building at the park.

The Final Phase of Land Transfers

In March, 1998, the final sale of land to the state occurred, designated as "Phase 3." The state now had title to somewhat more than the southern half of the park property, including the waterfront area containing the historic resort structures.

A half acre site for a Retreat Lodge was temporarily withheld from the transfer, under the assumption that the family would construct the building for the state as donation, after which the building and the land on which it sat would be handed over together. The county assessor, who had been notably uncooperative and unsympathetic throughout, immediately withdrew the parcel from its classification as forest land, resulting in a huge tax increase for the family. The family therefore deeded the piece to the state in December. It was later decided that the family would instead build and donate the Dining Hall, rather than the Retreat Lodge.

With the land transfers complete, the budgetary attentions now turned entirely to funding the capital development work and to paying for operating the park, including hiring a ranger for Cama Beach.

In May 1998, meetings were held at Cama Beach about transportation within the new park and at Burlington to prioritize the programs to be offered. Another meeting at the Puget Sound Region office in Auburn involved planning for the park in general. Participants included family members, Planning Manager Bill Koss, parks staff engineer Bill Tabor, and planner Paul Valcarce.

Funding the Two Major New Buildings

A Retreat Lodge had originally been proposed by the family, particularly Sandra and me, based on our many positive personal experiences at retreats. The quiet, relatively isolated natural ambience of Cama Beach seemed ideal for such a facility, where people could go to escape the pressures of daily life and renew themselves both physically and spiritually. The Retreat Lodge concept had been incorporated into the Master Plan and its updates with the assumption that it would be located on the shelf area slightly above the southern portion of the developed resort area, where four deluxe cabins had previously been sited (three of those cabins had burned in the 1950s, and the remaining cabin would be relocated below adjacent to the other deluxe cabins).

Originally, the family offered to pay for designing and building the Retreat Lodge. The other new building would be a Dining Hall, considered essential to provide meals to those staying overnight at the park, as well as day visitors who wished to purchase food. State Parks staff initially decided to fund the Dining Hall by the sale of Certificates of Participation (COPs), bonds that would be repaid, with interest, through revenues from operating the facility. However, after further financial analyses, it was doubtful that the Dining Hall operations could bring in sufficient revenues to repay the bonds.

The Retreat Lodge, however, appeared likely to be able to pay for itself though receipts from the rental of overnight accommodations and meeting rooms. Parks staff therefore asked if the family would be willing to "switch buildings," paying instead for the Dining Hall. Since we considered that building to be critically important to successful future park operations, we readily agreed.

The Dining Hall. During the development of the Master Plan, family members had enjoyed the contacts with the architectural consultants from the Miller/Hull firm of Seattle and were impressed with their work. The family therefore contacted partner Bob Hull in August 1998 and engaged Miller/Hull to do the design for the new Dining Hall. The building would be on the site of the former Recreation Hall that had burned in 1977, behind the double rows of waterfront cabins. Miller/Hull partner Craig Curtis would oversee the design process. Architects Rob Hutchison, Katie Popolow, and Renee Boone played major roles in the design over the following years, assisted at times by other staff.

Early in the process, it was decided that a two story structure would maximize the usefulness of the facility. The lower floor would contain the kitchen and a large dining room, which would have views of the water through the break in the rows of cabins. The dining room could also be used for large meetings and other gatherings in inclement weather. In good weather, the adjacent tennis court area on the south could serve as an outdoor eating area or as a space for interpretive lectures and performances. A long porch facing the water would provide covered outdoor space for relaxation.

The second floor would contain meeting rooms with a view of the water over the roofs of the cabins. One of those rooms would double as a reading room and casual lounge. At the rear would be four large, low-rent rooms for overnight accommodations, intended mainly for families and school and youth groups.

The architects held numerous meetings with the family, State Parks staff, and various consultants to refine the design. However, the proposal eventually ran into major archaeological obstacles which will be discussed later.

Formation of the Cama Beach State Park Advisory Committee

Those planning the park recognized that a somewhat unique approach was involved in that State Parks needed to work collaboratively with outside partners, particularly The Center for Wooden Boats, the Cama Beach Institute (still in existence at that time), and the family. So in August 1998 eleven participants gathered for an all day "Collaboration Retreat" at Saint Edward State Park, the former Catholic seminary on Lake Washington near Kirkland. It was a pleasant summer day, so most of the meeting was conducted outdoors around picnic tables.

A main result of the collaboration workshop was the formation of a "Cama Beach State Park Advisory Group" (referred to as the "Advisory Committee"), with formally designated representatives from each of the parties. The group would continue through the ensuing years as the main coordination body for the various entities involved in planning the park. Its first meeting was October 1, 1998, at The Center for Wooden Boats in Seattle, and this centrally located facility with its lovely location on Lake Union would become the usual venue for the future monthly meetings.

The meeting was chaired by Bill Koss, as would be most future gatherings for the next few years. He and Northwest Region Manager Terry Doran emphasized that the recommendations of the committee would have "great weight" with the agency.

Like any other entity wanting to do major development work on land, State Parks was required to apply for all relevant governmental permits. The attendees were informed that Alana Hess of the agency staff would be preparing the paperwork for the applications.

Probably the most exciting news at the meeting was that interviews would be conducted on October 12th for hiring the first ranger for Cama Beach. Howard Adams, the manager at Camano Island State Park, had been continuing to be in charge of Cama Beach also, assisted by ranger Roy Johnson. But clearly Cama needed someone focusing on it alone for security, for maintenance, and for handling any visitors. In recognition of the new park's importance, the position would be classified as a mid-level one, Ranger 3.

Frank Galloway, Cama Beach's First Ranger

On November 13, 1998, a "Ranger Welcome" party was held at Cama Home at Camano City, then the Hamalainen residence, to greet Frank Galloway, the new park manager. Enthusiastic and outgoing, and with numerous practical skills highly desirable for taking over a park with an aging infrastructure, Galloway was in many

ways an excellent fit for the job. His
wife Wendy and their two small
daughters moved to Camano Island,
and Wendy quickly became involved in
the local community.

Ongoing Park Planning

*An Economic Study and a Revised
Master Plan.* In March 1998, Tom
Oliva, recently hired Enterprise Coordinator for State Parks, developed an
economic feasibility study for the park
operations, titled *Resort Feasibility
Analysis.* The report surveyed market
trends and demographics and suggested some approaches to enhance the
revenue producing possibilities of the
park.

Frank Galloway, Cama Beach State Park's
first ranger/manager. (*Courtesy Washington
State Parks*)

In August 1998 a *Revised Concep-
tual Master Plan* was produced by State Parks' Puget Sound Resources Development
Office in Auburn. Primarily worked on by planner Paul Valcarce and engineer Bill
Tabor, the revisions made use of more recent information than was available to the
Atelier team for the original *Master Plan.* Most modifications did not affect the overall
concept or layout of the park, but a principal change was moving the upland parking areas to avoid affecting wetlands.

Other Park-Related Matters

Around this time, Arnie Larsen, an engineer on the State Parks staff with an
especially good aesthetic sense for designing buildings for parks and historical
settings, was assigned to do much of the design work at Cama Beach. It was expected
that he would also be on-site during much of the actual construction work.

Parks Planner Jim Ellis and Parks Environmental Specialist Chris Regan visited
Cama to delineate the edges of the wetlands and the buffers to help locate a route for
sections of the Cross-Island Trail on the Cama Beach land.

KING TV of Seattle sent a crew to Cama Beach to film a segment for its series
"Northwest Backroads." The segment aired a number of times in the ensuing
months and years.

Throughout 1998 and the following years, there were numerous meetings with
architects at Miller/Hull to plan the new Dining Hall to be funded by the family.

Meetings at State Parks headquarters in Olympia in late 1998 and early 1999 dealt with archaeological matters and historical and cultural-related plans.

Activities at the Legislature. In this period, as well as in later years, park advocates lobbied the Legislature for funding in virtually every session, with agency staff assisting by providing the capital budget requests and supporting information to the Legislature.

From to time to time FOCIP and CWB members in particular were called upon to voice support for the Cama Beach project before the Legislature or the State Parks and Recreation Commission. On a number of occasions active FOCIP members, including Carol Triplett, Pam Pritzl, John Edison, Howard Shuman, Don Hanna, Val Schroeder, Dave Eldridge and others either traveled to Olympia to testify before various panels or contacted legislators through phone calls, letters, and emails.

Larry Fairleigh, State Parks Assistant Director for Resource Development, talks of going from door to door at the Legislature session after session, and he mentions specifically the immense importance of Senator Mary Margaret Haugen's strong support.

A Sobering Flood. In late November 1998, Hugh Shipman, a coastal geologist with the state Department of Ecology's Northwest Region who was also an active Cama Beach Institute board member, visited Cama at a time of high winds and high tides. In a lengthy email, he noted seepage and ponding in low areas of the resort that appeared to be driven by high tides, including water covering around 90 % of the tennis court area and water flowing underneath, and out from under, the boat house. He doubted there was a simple fix to the problem.

On February 2, 1999, a combination of low atmospheric pressure and high tide resulted in flooding of the area from the deluxe cabins at the south end up to the front of the store on the north. A video by park manager Frank Galloway of the event was sobering. The water on the south end appeared to come from waves breaking over the seawall and was slow to drain away, while water near the boathouse came from a hole in the seawall. A hydrogeologist from AGRA Earth & Environmental of Kirkland, John Houck, made recommendations on how to minimize the problem in the future.

Eventually, in 2007, the problem would be dealt with in part by raising the cabins an average of one-and-one half feet on new foundation posts and hauling in around two hundred truck loads of fill which was spread in the lowest areas. Sea level rise due to global climate change may make these improvements even more relevant.

1990-91   Park Progress Timeline   **1999**   (2008 Opening)

The Retreat Lodge

In November 1998, a State Parks interview panel selected Leavengood Architects of Seattle to design the new Retreat Lodge. Beginning in January 1999, a series of meetings was held regarding the building's design, facilitated by architects Kate Johnson and David Leavengood, and involving the Cama Beach Advisory Committee and State Parks staff. The starting assumption, which remained throughout the design process, was that there would be fifteen double-occupancy rooms for overnight guests, as well as meeting rooms, a lounge area, and a small kitchen.

The family's original concept, and a preliminary sketch in the original master plan, was for a simple, relatively rustic facility with shared bathrooms for the overnight lodging rooms. This would be comparable to other basic-level retreat facilities such as those offered by some YMCA and church operated camps. In the actual design process, participants decided at the beginning that each room should have its own bathroom in keeping with modern preferences for individual convenience and privacy.

While still not in the "luxury" category, the Retreat Lodge design soon developed into a somewhat higher class of facility than the other buildings at the rustic historic resort. Family members expressed reservations about this change, in that the original intent was that the facility should be affordable for retreats by church groups and other nonprofit organizations, many of whose members could afford only relatively inexpensive venues. However, most participants in the planning process felt a facility with rooms comparable to those of a modern hotel was appropriate so as to offer a wider range of accommodations at the park. Cama Beach could then also cater to a clientele that was prepared to pay somewhat more for added comfort and better amenities, thus broadening the appeal of the facility while bringing in more rental income and repaying the COPs faster. It was hoped that this additional category of clientele would include those putting on events such as weddings and small business conferences, as well as individuals on "bed and breakfast" style vacations and honeymoons.

Continuing Park Related Events

The Master Plan is Updated. In May 1999, a meeting was held at the Puget Sound Regional Office in Auburn to discuss transportation to and within the park. A "Conceptual Master Plan" map was devised by Paul Valcarce, updating the earlier master plan developed by Atelier. The new plan depicted the parking lot and road layouts much closer to the final version eventually constructed.

A feature of both master plans was a day use area stretching the length of the beach in front of the bungalows at the north end of the resort. Picnic tables, a kitchen shelter, and even a small amphitheater were envisioned. Five of the original ten bungalows would be restored for uses which included meeting spaces and restrooms.

Later these plans for the bungalow area would be dropped due to concerns about the impact on the underlying Native American archaeological deposits; also, only two of the bungalows were in truly good enough condition for renovation and use.

Open Houses, FOCIP, and Trails. Also in May 1999, ranger Frank Galloway, with the assistance of FOCIP and The Center for Wooden Boats, began holding scheduled open houses to give the public a chance to see the park

Park Manager Frank Galloway with group of children. *(Courtesy Washington State Parks)*

property. Around 300 people attended the open house in May, and around 150 attended a later one.

Carol Triplett recounts how the FOCIP volunteers regularly worked Saturdays to maintain the grounds around the cabins during this period, in addition to helping host the open houses at which they set up displays about the park project and the history of Cama Beach.

Triplett also mentions the extensive efforts by FOCIP to construct trails, working in cooperation with State Parks and Island County. The Cross Island Trail was an early effort.

FOCIP work party near Cama Beach store in 1990s. Pictured: Pam Pritzl (left foreground); Kathy Haggerty (far left distance); believed to be Ole Eide (right foreground). *(Courtesy Carol Triplett, Friends of Camano Island Parks)*

There was also a feeling that walking along the beach should not be the main trail access to Cama, partly because of the private homes that would be affected. The county had sufficient right of way along the roads to accommodate a trail link between Camano Island State Park and Cama Beach, and eventually the county built that trail. A path across what is now the parking areas at Cama was also put in, but that trail has been superseded.

Historic and Cultural Discussions; the National Register Process. In the spring and summer of 1999, Advisory Committee meetings focused particularly on historic preservation at the park. Leavengood Architects, which had experience in this area, was hired to oversee this part of the project. Leavengood hired an experienced subconsultant, Florence "Flo" Lentz to assist. Kate Johnson and Lentz gave presentations to the Advisory Committee and facilitated the discussions.

As an aid to deliberations, Lentz and Johnson provided drafts of spreadsheet-style "Historical Resource Guidelines" listing the impacts to the historic resources of proposed new work, including modifications to specific existing areas and structures at the park, with various alternatives for how each should be treated and how the impacts of the work could be mitigated. The final column on the spreadsheets listed the conclusions based on the Advisory Committee discussions and the 1999 Conceptual Master Plan.

The end product , developed primarily by Flo Lentz, also included applications for National Historic Register and Washington Heritage Register status for the areas of the former Cama Beach Resort that were considered historically significant.

Dining Hall Concerns. Designs for the new Dining Hall and an adjacent Restroom/Bathhouse Building by Katie Popolow and Renee Boone of Miller/Hull were mostly completed. Around this time, Gerry Tays, historic preservationist on the State Parks staff, Karen Prasse of the Stanwood Area Historical Society, and others raised concerns about the effects of the new Dining Hall on the historic resort area. The two story building would be much larger than the adjacent existing 1930s structures and would clearly change the visual impact of the area.

Proponents of the Dining Hall argued that the new building was essential to the functioning of the park by conveniently providing needed food service and meeting rooms in a central location, as well as adding overnight accommodations for groups. They also pointed out that since the new building was to be constructed in the same location as the large Recreation Hall that had burned to the ground, it was merely taking the place of that former building.

The issue was eventually resolved in favor of continuing plans to build the Dining Hall, but the building was pushed back as far as possible toward the bluff, and extra efforts were made by the architects to minimize its size and design landscaping to soften its appearance, while retaining its important functions. Historic preservation staff continued to object strenuously to the planned new building as destroying the rare 1930s ambience of the resort area. As it later turned out, the building would in fact be relocated to a higher elevation due to archaeological concerns.

The Permitting and Planning Process Continues. On September 9, 1999, the agency's environmental specialist, Alana Hess, sent a twelve page "Pre-Application Submittal" to Island County, outlining the proposed park development, and a meeting with the county staff was scheduled for October 28th.

At the September Advisory Group meeting, Rob Hutchison of Miller/Hull presented a floor plan and elevations for the proposed Dining Hall and Bathhouse. An attached time line indicated an eight month construction period that would begin in March and end in November 2000.

The committee was given a tentative time table for opening the park, with a Grand Opening scheduled for April 1, 2001. Reservations for accommodations would be taken beginning in April 2000.

Soon, unanticipated events would make those plans impractical. It would take an additional six years beyond the projected dates before the park could open to the public.

Archaeological Explorations and Tribal Concerns

Federally recognized Native American tribes are sovereign nations, and the appropriate protocol for a state agency's initial contacts with a tribe, and for major communications or discussions that follow, is for the head of the agency to approach the president or chair of the tribe's board of directors. Parks and Recreation Commissioner Joan Thomas now says, "In the beginning some of the agency staff didn't understand the need for formal government-to-government communication with the tribes. They assumed that any agency staff person could talk with a tribal representative and it would be adequate consultation."

It was standard procedure for State Parks to send notifications of permit applications and other significant development activities to any Native American tribes who could have an interest in the project. In early 2000 the agency applied to the state Office (now Department) of Archaeology and Historic Preservation (OAHP) for limited digging to explore the possibility of any underlying archaeological deposits, commonly referred to under the term "cultural resources," and to ensure that if any existed, they would not be harmed by the development work. A Native American grave had been discovered in 1999, and the clearance for beginning the archaeological work was slowed due to concerns expressed by the Swinomish Tribe about adequate measures for protecting any additional discoveries. OAHP at last issued a permit allowing digging at Cama with certain

procedures and protocols in place in case more artifacts or other sensitive items were found. However, according to a State Parks document, the permit process had delayed the project fourteen months.

Early in 2000, Dan Meatte, State Parks staff archaeologist, and Park Manager Frank Galloway met with tribal representatives on site at Cama. Hank Gobin attended from the Tulalip Tribes and Larry Campbell represented the Swinomish. Galloway felt at the time that the tribes appeared willing to cooperate with the park project, and Meatte was drafting up procedures to be agreed upon. The Swinomish Tribe expressed an intent to have an observer present during the construction work.

Separately, the Upper Skagit Tribe expressed interest in harvesting shellfish at Cama in accordance with treaty rights, and they were to be allowed to do so on part of the beach with certain poundage limits. There would be an annual evaluation of the health of the beach by the State Parks stewardship manager.

Over seven years followed with many meetings between State Parks and interested tribes, delays in the park project resulting from concerns raised by tribal representatives, and in some instances, tribal legal appeals of issuance of the needed permits. The sections later in this book that deal with those matters are extremely abbreviated summaries of what occurred.

Parametrix is Hired for the Park's Design and Engineering

Interviews of four finalists were held in December 1999 to select a firm to do the actual design of the entire park, including detailed construction drawings. Bremerton-based Parametrix (PMX) was chosen. On January 10, 2000, at the beginning of the "new millennium," the recently hired Parametrix design team was introduced to the Advisory Committee. Attending were Diane Lenius, Project Manager; Curt Warber, landscape architect; Gary Maynard, who would coordinate the SEPA work and permitting; Dick Metler, architect with the PMX subsidiary, Meritt+Pardini; and John Burk, civil engineer. Lenius would continue enthusiastic involvement with the project until the ultimate opening of the park, as would Warber.

The extent of the task Parametrix had taken on was becoming clear. An organization chart for the "Cama Beach Project Team" numbered at least 38 individuals among the consultants; at least six State Parks staff; and the citizen Advisory Committee members, of which there were six or more who regularly attended the meetings.

Parametrix would continue to be involved in designing and overseeing construction for at least the next seven years. Parks Planning and Research Manager Bill Koss remembers Parametrix as bringing "a lot of clever solutions" to the project in dealing with such concerns as storm water, utility placement, and raising the buildings." Koss also recalls that with the involvement of Parametrix and its expertise, there was an "epiphany" when the State Parks staff realized that the amount of money needed for the project was much more than previously envisioned.

Diane Lenius, Managing Principal of the project for Parametrix throughout the firm's involvement, was passionate about the park from the very beginning. She recalls, "Every time you went to the site, you knew it was important." She remembers "feeling good about what we were trying to do" and that she was personally excited to be the Project Manager. She also recalls being aware that "there were expectations to live up to," including carrying out the donor family's vision for the park.

Parametrix has a wide range of expertise on its staff, but Lenius says, "The project challenged every asset of the company: environmental, architectural, permitting, working with the county." Listing a few of the wide range of specific tasks Parametrix was involved in at Cama that it also does on other consulting jobs, such as building roads, taking care of a dump site, and permitting, she emphasizes, "We don't have the opportunity on the other projects to do the work for a place with the *meaning* that Cama Beach has."

The National Register Listing, and the Secretary of the Interior's Guidelines

In early 2000, the resort area was placed on both the National Register of Historic Places and the Washington Heritage Register. A letter afterwards from Washington Secretary of State Ralph Munro to Parks Director Pinnix says, "I was so pleased and delighted . . . I think Cama Beach is one of our 'classics' and something that we will remember with pride for many years in the future."

The agency's *Cultural Resources Management Policy*, which had been adopted in 1998, states that for properties placed on the National Register, "as general guidance for work on any historic structures . . . the Commission will use the Secretary of the Interior's 'Standards for the Treatment of Historic Properties with Guidelines for Preserving, Rehabilitating, Restoring and Reconstructing Historic Buildings.'" In the ensuing years, these guidelines would in fact govern the rehabilitation work on the structures at Cama Beach.

Center for Wooden Boats Activity. Meanwhile, the long term agreement between The Center for Wooden Boats and State Parks was being worked on. The Cama Beach Advisory Committee continued to hold most of its monthly meetings at the CWB facility on South Lake Union in Seattle. No one expected that it would be 2008 before the formal agreement between CWB and the state would finally be signed.

By the late 1990s CWB member Rich Kolin had been involved with the organization for some time, including a period on the board as vice-president with an emphasis on Cama Beach, and later as a representative on the Cama Beach State Park Advisory Committee. Kolin says there were volunteers in the Camano Island area who were interested in CWB, but some had never owned a wooden boat. So he began offering boat building classes, largely as an orientation for the volunteers. Cama Beach was not yet available for use as a venue, but like others involved, Kolin assumed it would only be a couple of years until the park opened. He began offering classes where he lived near Marysville to be relatively close to the Camano area volunteers.

Under his instruction and using his own designs, students built boats ranging from 12 feet in length through 18 feet, intended for CWB's rental fleet at Cama Beach. Kolin says that the flat bottomed skiffs and the wherries were especially appropriate for launching from the beach, and "the skiffs are particularly good for rental boats, as they are stable and fast, lending themselves well to rowing." Since the boats were rarely totally completed during the classes, Kolin typically finished them himself. Eventually, as a result of the classes, the fleet ended up with thirteen boats and ten sets of oars (unfortunately, three boats were later crushed by falling trees during a windstorm at the park).

With grants from Karen Hamalainen, Kolin also measured and made blueprints of all eight types of the historic Cama Beach Resort Boats. Because the old resort boats were in various degrees of deterioration and it was not practical to restore them for actual use, three or four were painted for display purposes only, and he and his class built three new replicas to use at the park.

Furnishings for the Park. Allison Alderman, who developed the budgets for the Northwest Region office, was successful in getting approval of a generous allowance purchase of furnishings for the new park. Sandra Worthington began purchasing bedspreads or quilts and area rugs for the fifteen Retreat Lodge overnight rooms, utilizing her knowledge of fabrics from lifelong sewing experience.

Hiring Additional Staff. In August of 2000, Melanie Ford Bissey was hired for the position, awkwardly titled, "Parks & Recreation Coordinator 1 – In training for Conference Program Supervisor" (much later, the position was changed to "Conference Coordinator"). Melanie was already a highly thought of employee of State Parks. She had organized a successful festival at Fort Worden State Park, and she had prior interpretive experience with the National Park Service at the Arizona Memorial in Hawaii. Although interpretative programs had been her main focus, an Interpretive Specialist position as such was not yet available for Cama Beach, and she found she liked being involved with the tourism and travel management aspects of the new position.

Around the same time, Richard Donovan was hired as Construction and Maintenance Project Specialist 1, a position commonly known in the park system as a "C & M." He brought a wealth of practical experience and skills to the challenging job of maintaining the old resort structures.

It was assumed that additional staff would soon be hired, but due to the subsequent extended delays resulting from archaeological issues, Ford Bissey and Donovan would become the only permanent staff persons at Cama Beach for the next seven years, aside from park manager Galloway and his eventual successor Jeff Wheeler.

Design Considerations. Parametrix staff came up with four alternative roadway and parking layouts that were presented for consideration by landscape architect Curt Warber at the Advisory Committee meeting in October 2000. The objectives of the layouts were to maintain the forest canopy and historic character, reduce walking distances, provide good vehicular and pedestrian circulation, and provide adequate storm water treatment. The consensus was that the preferred option was one in which the entry road would parallel the top of the bluff. This option was eventually adopted and constructed.

In the October meeting the new sewage, water, and storm water systems were also discussed. The drain field for the sewage would be on the east side of the county road, necessitating pumping the effluent a long distance and to a higher elevation. The 85,000 gallon tank for drinking water would also be on the east side of the county road, at a high elevation to ensure proper water pressure.

A New Park Manager, Jeff Wheeler

Despite the construction delays resulting from tribal concerns, other events related to the park were continuing. In early 2001, Camano Island State Park and Cama Beach State park were reorganized into a "Cama Beach Area," with Camano Island State Park considered a "satellite" to Cama due to the latter's upcoming importance as a major destination park. A new Area Manager position was created, and the post was open to competition from within the ranks for the rangers. At the beginning of March 2001, Jeff Wheeler, an experienced senior ranger, was selected for the post, placing him in direct supervisory charge of Cama Beach, as well as of Camano Island State Park.

Jeff Wheeler, Cama Beach State Park Area Manager

Wheeler says he applied for the position because "I grew up at Fort Worden State Park, and I saw a magical place there with its partnership with Centrum. I saw a chance to do that again at Cama," and maybe to avoid some of the problems through the lessons learned at Fort Worden. "I also wanted a big, busy park, with exciting new things happening."

1990-91   Park Progress Timeline   **2001**   (2008 Opening)

Jeff, his wife Laurie, and the two children moved into the house at Cama Beach, where they stayed for two and a half years, until they moved into ranger housing at Camano Island State Park.

Frank Galloway's main duties were shifted to Camano Island State Park. He applied for other jobs in the system and ended up pleased with a position at State Park headquarters in Olympia, including, some years later, implementing the new statewide "No Child Left Inside" grant program.

Funding in the 2001 Legislative Session

The family had pledged an amount in cash donations that was originally considered adequate for the new Dining Hall and adjacent Bathhouse building, but with newly refined budget information, it had become clear as the year progressed that funds on hand would not be sufficient for the extensive work needing to be done. It was thought that if enough additional funds were appropriated, the park could open in 2002.

As the 2001 legislative session drew near, the state's financial situation did not look good. Governor Gary Locke required state agencies to come up with proposals to cut their operating budgets by 4%. This would affect any new hires at Cama, and it also made it more difficult to ask for the needed $4 million capital appropriation.

It is always much easier for proponents if a budget item is included early in the process, rather than having to try to convince key legislators to insert the funds later. It was a huge disappointment for Cama Beach supporters when the Governor's proposed budget came out without any capital funding whatsoever for Cama Beach. The budget also proposed delaying staff funding for Cama for two years. Influential Senator Haugen immediately fired off a press release titled "Some Things Aren't Open to Compromise" to alert the media to the problem. In the release she stated, "Getting Cama Beach State Park staffed and running is one of my top priorities this legislative session. Anyone who has ever been there will understand why."

Park proponents began an intensive lobbying effort. I consulted State Parks' legislative liaison, Rex Derr (who later become Director of State Parks), and also professional lobbyist James L. "Jim" King, Jr., who had long been an ardent supporter of outdoor recreation causes. King had recently formed a loose coalition called Citizens for Parks and Recreation. His expertise on park and recreation budget matters is unparalleled, and he would become a key figure in lobbying for Cama Beach funding over the next several legislative sessions.

We were also fortunate in that Mike Ryherd, an experienced lobbyist who regularly worked for conservation groups and had helped the Cama Beach effort in the past, willingly volunteered his assistance. In combination with Jim King it was a terrific team. Ryherd formulated a plan in which the Cama supporters would use the family's offer of its cash donation, in addition to the land donations, as an incentive for the Legislature to appropriate the requested added funds.

On February 28, 2001, with the Legislature in session, a serious earthquake hit the state capitol area. The Legislative Building had to be closed, and space needed to be found for the lawmakers in adjacent buildings. With the state facing the costs of earthquake repairs, the budget was even tighter.

I prepared a flyer for legislators summarizing exactly what the needed funds would be used for and including photos of the park. Karen Hamalainen had Miller/Hull architects prepare a brochure with an attractive rendering of the proposed Dining Hall and Bath House.

I also circulated an email to Cama Beach supporters with the Cama budget request details, and with contact information for legislators throughout the northern Puget Sound area. Park supporters, especially on Camano Island, as well as Center for Wooden Boats members, sent emails and letters to legislators asking for full capital funding for Cama Beach.

This was a session in which the state House of Representatives was equally divided between Republicans and Democrats, which meant that each committee in had split chairmanships. Fortunately, the park advocates had some key supporters in the House. Representative Sehlin of Oak Harbor, a strong supporter of parks in general and Cama Beach in particular, was Republican co-chair of House Appropriations. Representative Barlean of Langley was Republican Vice-Chair of Appropriations and also had a seat on the Capital Budget Committee.

Representatives Gary Alexander, Republican from Olympia, and Ed Murray, Democrat from Seattle, were Co-chairs of the House Capital Budget Committee. One of my most vivid memories of the long legislative session was an evening at home in April when I acted as something of an intermediary, exchanging a number emails with Rep. Murray and with Republican Co-chair Alexander, passing on to each of them the other's assurances of willingness to fund the full $4 million. But it wasn't until June when the seemingly interminable session finally ended that we were finally guaranteed the funding was secure.

The Permit Process and Tribal Archaeological Appeals

In the fall of 2000, the Tulalip Tribes appealed the issuance by DAHP of the permit allowing archaeological work at Cama Beach and also requested to have an observer present during the digging. It was anticipated that the archaeological field work would take a couple weeks, plus additional analysis off-site. The work would be undertaken by a reputable consultant, Dr. Randall Schalk of Cascadia Archaeology of Seattle.

Contacts continued in 2001 between the agency and tribal representatives in an effort to work out an agreement on locating the proposed utility trenches, with State Parks suggesting relocating the main utility line at the toe of the slope to try to minimize any disturbance of the archaeological deposits in the ground. Bill Koss met with Hank Gobin and Terry Williams of the Tulalip Tribes and scheduled an additional meeting with Larry Campbell of the Swinomish. His impression from the

Tulalip meeting was that the tribe was strongly interested in interpretation programs at Cama. However, the Tulalips also wanted to be the exclusive tribe for doing the interpretation.

Joan Thomas, a member of the Parks and Recreation Commission during this period recalls when she and Commissioner Petersen, Commissioner Mickey Fearn, Director Rex Derr, and Assistant Director Larry Fairleigh met for the first time with the Tulalip Tribal Council. She believes "it was fruitful, even though there was no definite outcome."

It was exciting for those involved in the park project to learn that Randall Schalk and his team from Cascadia Archaeology carbon dated fire-blackened rocks from a pit at the proposed site for the new dining building to use as a fire ring between 1400 and 1600 years ago. Cascadia's web site briefly summarized their efforts, stating: "The scope of work involved augering, excavation of shovel probes, and larger test excavation units to evaluate the integrity and significance of a shell midden deposit that lies beneath the resort. The testing effort revealed that the deeply stratified midden deposits span at least the last 16 centuries, contain an abundance of vertebrate and invertebrate faunal remains, and retain a high degree of archaeological integrity."

SEPA Compliance. Meanwhile, in April 2001, to comply with the State Environmental Policy Act (SEPA), State Parks issued a "Mitigated Determination of Non-Significance" signed by SEPA Official Alana Hess with respect to the work to be done at Cama. This was a determination that there would be no probable significant adverse impact on the environment, and hence no formal Environmental Impact Statement (EIS) need be issued, a considerable saving in staff time and costs. In particular, the only clearing of trees and other vegetation would be the minimum needed for the new parking areas and roads, and there would be a new sewage system and also improvements to control any storm water runoff.

Shoreline Permit Approval; and Tulalip Concerns. On September 6, 2001, the Island County hearing examiner approved the park project's Shoreline Substantial Development Permit, pursuant to the state Shoreline Management Act. This was major news, as the Shoreline Permit was the "umbrella" permit under which the other county approvals would be granted. Some conditions were placed on the approval, the most significant of which was that State Parks must meet with the interested tribes and obtain an archaeological excavation permit prior to any excavation work.

The Tulalip Tribes filed an appeal of the decision, apparently prematurely. On September 20 a meeting was held with several representatives of the Tulalip Tribes, State Parks staff, and various consultants on the project including archaeological consultant Randall Schalk. Little was resolved at that time. But it had become clear the Tulalips wanted the project to proceed more slowly; that they were asserting their sole right to the Cama Beach area; and that they viewed other tribes as having no claim on the Cama Beach land. This created considerable awkwardness for State Parks in future discussions and negotiations, as the agency is legally required to treat all interested tribes similarly and does not have the authority to decide that only certain ones have valid claims to a site. The Tulalip representatives also expressed a desire, which would be repeated in later years, that the land be returned to them, if not as a gift, than as a purchase.

As former owners still actively involved in the project, we realized it would be good to do more to establish a personal relationship with the tribes. In January 2002, Sandra and I visited Tulalip Cultural Resources manager Hank Gobin. It was clear that Mr. Gobin had serious concerns about the possibility of more undiscovered graves at Cama Beach. Yet, we had the impression that he would be open to the possibility of some interpretation of tribal history at Cama. His enthusiasm for traditional ocean-going canoes had come out during the meeting, and we left hoping this interest might eventually lead to some form of regular event at Cama Beach involving Native American watercraft.

State Parks Director Pinnix sent a letter to the tribal chairs of the Tulalips and the Swinomish, requesting that they agree to a protocol for assessing whether there were any archaeological concerns in the forested area where the parking lots were to be developed and in the Retreat lodge site. State Parks hoped this process would open the way for development work on the upper elevations, even if work was stalled in the waterfront area.

In early January 2002, after he and his crew had worked in some difficult winter weather, including high winds, Randall Schalk completed a report on the sampling in the plateau area of the proposed parking lots and found little of archaeological concern.

Both the archaeological explorations and State Parks' contacts with the tribes continued. In March, another tribe showed strong interest when the chairman and vice-chairman of the Stillaguamish visited Cama Beach.

Formal Appeal of the Shoreline Permit.

On April 15, 2002, the Shoreline Substantial Development Permit was formally issued by Island County, subject to conditions that included adopting a cultural resources treatment plan to be reviewed by the county, the Office of Archaeology and Historic Preservation, and the Tulalip and Swinomish tribes.

On the last day of the time period for interested parties to challenge the issuance of the permit, the Tulalip Tribes filed a formal appeal to the state Shoreline Hearings Board, based primarily on the impact of the proposed construction work on the underlying archaeological deposits. The board would have 180 days to consider the appeal and render its decision, with a potential appeal of that decision to Superior Court.

The appeal resulted in halting almost all work on the project again, with the hearing scheduled for early October. Meanwhile, Barbara Herman, the Assistant Attorney General assigned to represent State Parks on the matter, made efforts to resolve the issues and settle the appeal.

In August 2002, State Parks and the Tulalip Tribes entered into an agreement dismissing the appeal to the Shoreline Hearings Board, but including a number of provisions. The other interested tribes were not involved in the appeal and were therefore not parties to the agreement. Among the main matters agreed upon, the Tulalip Tribes acknowledged the sufficiency of the treatment plan devised by State Parks for avoiding damage to, and dealing with, archaeological artifacts and human remains, and the tribe was entitled to have a trained observer present during construction. State Parks agreed it would not develop the northern portion of the bungalow area of the waterfront part of the resort. This was a significant concession, as it removed a major portion of the planned day use area from future recreational activities.

The Tulalips were given the right to construct an interpretive center in the form of a long house, open to the public, to convey the history and archaeological connection to the site of Native Americans. The location would be subject to State Parks' approval, and the Tribe would pay all costs. State Parks would grant a fifty year, no cost lease for the site. The provision for the long house would be subject to cancellation by State Parks if construction did not begin within five years (the time period did in fact expire with no action taken by the Tribe regarding the long house).

According to a State Parks document, the project was delayed an additional eight months as a result of the need to resolve this particular appeal. Tribal concerns were manifested again in subsequent years; those will be taken up later in this narrative.

Park-Related Interim Events, 2002-2005

Staff Transitions. In August 2002, Jeanne Wahler was hired as Capital Project Manager for the Northwest Region. She would continue in that role over the next several years through the park opening, later under the title of Parks Development Region Manager. An email from Bill Koss to the Advisory Group and others stated that he was "transitioning from managing the Cama Beach project in order to devote 100% of my time to managing the Planning and Research Program." He wrote, "The past 6 plus years has been a stupendously gratifying period. Using the skills and passion of a number of people we took the original Master plan and made it into a living document that will guide the park for a long time . . . And we now have blueprints and permits for starting the construction." In Appendix 2 to this book, part of that same email is reproduced in which Koss reviews the names of many who contributed significantly to the project.

Jeanne Wahler had heard of Cama Beach as a "big project" for the agency, with some of the staff obviously tired of the problems and delays. "It was an albatross for some," she says. But Wahler "didn't have that baggage," nor did Mike Allen, hired around the same time as Capital Program Manager at the State Parks headquarters in Olympia, and Wahler's immediate supervisor.

Wahler received the massive set of files from Bill Koss and realized it was "such a big project, and I hadn't taken on anything like it before." However, she "likes challenges and dealing with multiple stakeholders." Working on the project was often a struggle for those in the agency, "but everyone was saying they still wanted to do this, and that it would be a really good thing when it was done." She spoke of "the magic of it, and how a *place* can drive people."

Wahler subsequently began chairing the Advisory Committee Meetings, taking over that task from Koss. Jeanne's assistant, Marsha Harvey, began taking notes at the meetings and compiling the minutes. Wahler would report to Mike Allen on capital budget and program matters, and he in turn would report to Assistant Director Larry Fairleigh.

In September 2002, with the retirement of Cleve Pinnix, the Commission selected Rex Derr to be the new Director of State Parks. Widely liked and respected, Derr had served as legislative liaison and in other posts for the agency, in addition to an earlier stint as Mayor of Olympia.

The "Groundbreaking." After so many years of effort by so many people to bring the park into being, it seemed appropriate to have a celebration. So on October 30, 2002, a "Groundbreaking Ceremony" was held at Cama Beach in anticipation of the first capital construction work starting soon.

The Park is Officially Named. Occasionally, the former owners would be asked if they would like the new park named after the family. But family members were unanimous in asserting that since "Cama Beach" was the name that had become familiar to everyone since the 1930s, that name was by far the most appropriate one to use. At its meeting in Olympia on December 12, 2002, the State Parks and Recreation Commission formally adopted the name of "Cama Beach State Park."

Efforts to Buy Additional Land. Around this time, efforts were made to buy a thirty acre parcel that had become available adjacent to Cama Beach land on the east side of the county road. The property would make an excellent addition to the park as it would protect a portion of the creek area and would also provide an desirable site for the proposed ranger housing and shop buildings. It was also conveniently situated between the two state parks. However, the owner eventually decided not to deal with the agency after all, and the negotiations ended. Park supporters, however, continued to hope that eventually the important piece could be acquired.

1990-91   Park Progress Timeline   **2003**   (2008 Opening)

The Business Plan. Those planning the park and lobbying for funding had recognized for some time that it would be important to have a formal, detailed business plan for the park and its operations. In the fall of 2003, State Parks contracted with the Small Business Development Center of Western Washington University's College of Business and Economics to develop the plan. A team under the direction of Thomas Dorr worked intensively on the plan, and a final draft came out in February 2004, in time for that year's short legislative session.

The Cama Beach Quilters, and the Furniture Makers. A group of talented quilters began meeting regularly at Cama Beach to work on making quilts, with the ambitious goal of donating a hundred quilts to the park. The gorgeous quilts have periodically been displayed at events at Cama and elsewhere. The Cama Beach Quilters later also took on sewing curtains for the cabin windows.

The Cama Beach Furniture Makers, experienced volunteer woodworkers, also lent their impressive expertise to the park, making numerous pieces of furniture including thirty benches for outside the cabins, twenty-four Adirondack chairs, thirty tables for the cabins, and a large number of picnic tables and benches.

How Those Involved Dealt with the Long Process

During the long process of park development, Jeff Wheeler, in addition to speaking to local community groups such as the Kiwanis, Lions, and Rotary, took on participation in Island County Beach Watchers and membership in FOCIP. He was also on a county-wide trails planning committee, and he became involved with the Whidbey-Camano Land Trust.

Wheeler now says regarding the project delays, "A lot of it was difficult, but it gave the staff a huge chance to learn more about the park, about the family, and CWB. It also gave us a chance to get involved more with the local community, as we didn't have to spend all our time running the park on a day to day basis." As a result, "Cama Beach has more partnerships than any other park in the system, because of so much time to interact with the community."

The staff also used the period to make contact with other organizations that expect to partner with Cama for programs, including the North Cascades Institute, the Mountaineers, and operators of the historic ship replica, *Lady Washington*.

An unanticipated aspect of Conference Coordinator Melanie Ford Bissey's job was the necessity of moving her office many times: from the house at Cama into two adjoining deluxe cabins, then out of one of the cabins, then to Camano Island State Park during much of the Phase 2B construction, next to the newly completed Welcome Station, and finally to a hoped-for permanent location in the house on the waterfront. "It was hard to know when packing up what I would need, and how long it would be in storage." Items such as catalogs for purchasing furniture and equipment for the park that were expected to be in storage for six months instead ended up being packed away and unavailable for three years.

She speaks of the halts and the delays in park development over the years as "very frustrating." With the park not expected to be in operation soon, her job classification that anticipated coordinating a conference center was not a good fit for the routine administrative work that ended up occupying so much of her time.

She says that during the long delays she came to view her mission as "being a cheerleader for Cama Beach." She and Jeff Wheeler made it their jobs to try to help keep the local public informed of the status of the park project, "answering questions positively and honestly," and to keep jobs lined up for the many volunteers who were eager to help at the park. Wheeler's presentations to community groups often attracted volunteers to the park, and typically Ford Bissey then coordinated much of the volunteers' work.

She became active in the Stanwood Chamber of Commerce and in 2006 helped launch the Snow Goose Festival. She was involved with the county tourism board which coordinated tourism promotion, funded by a 2% hotel/motel tax. She feels in the process she "got the park a lot of free marketing." She also later took on a two year commitment within State Parks as a member of the director's Leadership Team as one of three staff pulled in from the field, giving her an opportunity to know upper management staff better and to gain a familiarity with statewide park issues.

Dick Wagner of The Center for Wooden Boats says, "The only troublesome part for me about the delays was that people kept asking when Cama Beach would open. I'd tell them a date, and then the date would get changed again to later."

The delays were difficult for Allison Alderman, Assistant Northwest Region Manager for Human and Financial Resources. Her job covers putting together the operating budget requests for Cama Beach, including funding the proposed staff positions and the initial "one time" equipment and furnishings purchases, with justifications for every item. In the beginning, after a long process, she was pleased that she was able to obtain the entire amounts asked for. But with the delays, the money was taken back.

As the years went on with more delays the budget had to be continually updated for inflation and cost of living increases for salaries, then resubmitted, often two or three times per year, with items split up into categories that frequently changed. Headquarters budget staff often changed, as did Office of Financial Management (OFM) personnel and legislative staffers. Alderman had to go through the justification process over and over again. New staff people had to be educated so they understood the project and the vision. Then, the next postponements meant it was necessary to do the education process yet again. But, Alderman says, "Cama Beach is a great place, and when I'd go down there I'd get re-energized and excited about the project again."

She particularly recalls hosting a meeting of her counterparts from other regions at Cama Beach a few years before the park opening. The participants stayed in the cabins and met in the house. After going out to dinner, they returned to Cama and sat around a campfire. She says, "Everyone remembers it as a great experience, and one of the most productive meetings was the conversation around the fire."

The Active Volunteer Summit. Numerous volunteers assisted at various projects at Cama Beach over the years, both with outdoor work and in the office. To recognize the various individuals and groups involved, Jeff Wheeler and the park staff organized an "Active Volunteer Summit" held at Cama on June 19, 2004. The day was sunny and pleasant, and after a potluck picnic lunch, groups were given five minutes each to tell about their activities. The fourteen organizations, and the persons speaking for them, are listed in Appendix 2.

Gathering of active volunteers for a picnic and presentations at Cama Beach, June 2004. Quilts by the Cama Beach Quilters group are displayed on the bungalow porch railing. *(Courtesy Washington State Parks and Recreation Commission)*

State Senator Mary Margaret Haugen spoke and was honored with a plaque by Jim King, Jr., of Olympia on behalf of Citizens for Parks and Recreation, the statewide lobbying group he coordinates. The award recognized her continuing efforts on behalf of Cama Beach and parks in general. Representative Hans Dunshee was unable to come, but he later received a similar plaque. As a souvenir of the event for those attending, Melanie Ford Bissey came up with a half dozen refrigerator magnets, each with a color photo depicting an aspect of Cama Beach. Years later, attendees occasionally still mention having the magnets on their refrigerators.

Betsy Davis, recently hired as Executive Director of The Center for Wooden Boats, saw Cama Beach for the first time that day. "It felt like a magic place," she says. "It's such a beautiful place on the water. It's as close to being on a boat as you can get without actually being on one." She also remembers, "The spirit of the volunteers was something special. Everybody was so active and enthused."

Construction of Parking, Roads, and Utilities (Phase 1)

After sample digs in the higher elevations above the waterfront by Cascadia Archaeology, it had been agreed by tribal representatives that this portion of the park was not likely to have archaeological significance. In late 2003, construction began at last on the upper parking lots and utilities by Strider Construction of Bellingham, with Ben Hudson as its project manager.

Designated as "Phase 1," the extensive work included the paved access road and parking areas with the accompanying lighting; the new water system with its 85,000 gallon reservoir tank on a high elevation east of the county road; and new underground electrical lines and sewage piping to a distance of 200 feet from the shoreline.

The Entry Roads and Parking Areas. Landscape architect Curt Warber of Parametrix says the entry road along the bluff before entering the parking bays "was designed to give folks a pleasant experience of Cama before going into the parking lots, so coming into the park wouldn't be defined by seeing hundreds of cars in a lot." Fellow landscape architect Jens Swenson speaks of first "experiencing the light coming in through the trees on the bluff, and then finding the best option for parking."

Because the parking areas are spread out, the designers tried to reduce the stress of deciding where to park by using a principle of "load for the closest first." Visitors initially drive to the parking area nearest to the top of the bluff above the waterfront, adjacent to the drop-off shelter and waiting area. If the closer spots are all taken, drivers then head farther away (after first unloading passengers and belongings, if they wish) until they find a place to park, but they will know that they are nevertheless in the nearest available spot to where they want to end up.

Damon McAlister, the engineer in charge as overall project manager for Parametrix after Diane Lenius, was on site an average of once a week during construction. "The work went relatively smoothly," he says. Although many trees had to be removed to make room for the parking areas and roads, both State Parks and Parametrix went to considerable effort to try to save larger, more significant trees, including relocating utilities and changing roadway alignments when needed. "We tried to keep as much of the character as possible of the upper area," McAlister says, "even working to save stumps with springboard notches from the early logging days." The usable wood from the removed trees has been stored at Camano Island State Park, as a source for making furniture and other items for the parks.

Efforts were made to use existing flat areas as much as possible for parking. Landscape architect Warber also says, "We feel we made reasonable buffers between the parking areas. And if we did our job well, the forest will heal itself and will come back to the edge of the facilities."

At the top of the steep hill down to the water, it was necessary to cut into the slopes more. Warber says, "We made a decision to use a lot of rock walls, rather than to cut and fill slopes and lay open more of the landscape. The access road to the Retreat Lodge site was frustrating, as it had to be so steep, and we couldn't reduce the scale. The grading was more intensive than we'd wanted. But we hope it will heal up and feel more integrated after the building construction is completed."

Jens Swenson speaks of the impressive effort to preserve native plants during the process. "We saved over 2,500 sword ferns, many a hundred years old or so." The plants were stored by the roadway leading up to the water tank during construction. They were then brought back to the new roads and parking areas and used for landscape restoration. New container plants, all native vegetation such as snowberry, ocean spray, and shrub rose, were also used for the roadside landscape to meld the cleared areas into the uncleared.

The Lighting. In designing the parking lot lighting, Warber felt some frustration at trying to find lights which fit the character of the old resort and blended well with the site. Custom designed lights would have required a six month UL (Underwriters Laboratory) process for approval. "It's amazing how poor the choices are for off-the-shelf lighting," he says. But he feels that in the end the character of the tall light standards turned out fairly well. "If the fixtures had been lower, we'd have ended up with twice as many. And it's a balance between too much light and providing enough lighting so people can feel safe, as well as finding their cars and keeping track of their children." The fixtures were also chosen to direct the light down onto the parking lot, without a lot of spillover into general glare and illumination of the night sky.

Warber is personally less pleased with the trail lighting, feeling the short wood light standards are "chunkier than I'd have preferred, as the character isn't similar to the 'small sticks' of the old resort." But it was necessary to make them sturdy to hold up under public use and long term effects of the weather. Colleague Jens Swenson, on the other hand, likes the trail lamp bollards, feeling "they invite people to walk along the alignment."

The New Utility Systems. A huge amount of engineering design work, construction effort, and expensive infrastructure is buried in the earth, where few visitors will ever be aware of it. Once leaving West Camano Drive, the electrical and communications wiring is all underground, where it is protected from the frequent winter

Septic tanks prior to installation in ground, 2005.

wind storms, as well as being out of sight so as to not interfere with the scenic beauty.

For the new park water system, well water from the west side of the county road is pumped in underground pipes eastward up to the 85,000 gallon reservoir tank, and the water then drains by gravity back down to the buildings in the parking areas and the waterfront area. Sewage is pumped upward from the waterfront area, past the parking lot area buildings, and then easterly to the drain fields on the far side of the road.

The utility pipes obviously needed to cross West Camano Drive. During construction, an excavation was done under the roadway and a large steel pipe pushed through, without breaking the surface of the pavement. The utility lines were then pulled through this larger pipe.

The drain fields for the sewage system were constructed in "Phase 2A" by another contractor, Earthwise Excavation of Snohomish. Illustrative of the care taken for the project, Damon McAlister points out that at a relatively late date the Parametrix engineers changed the design to a "subsurface drip system," which was newly approved by the Department of Health. The new design not only caused much less impact to tree roots, it was also less costly.

It was also necessary to install a sewer line on the east side of the county road, from a point opposite the main park entrance running eastward a thousand feet until connecting to the drain field. To minimize the environmental impact, a "horizontal direction drilling" approach was used, involving boring eight to fifteen feet under the wetlands and under the tree root zone.

The 2004 Legislative Session

Representative Hans Dunshee of Snohomish was an early, enthusiastic supporter of the park project. An avid kayaker and parks user, his first view of Cama Beach had been after launching his kayak at Camano Island State Park and paddling north: "I came to this mysterious place, with a long, undeveloped beach. The buildings were in a sorry state, but it was still enchanting. When I got a chance to help bring it into public ownership, it was an easy thing to support. The number of places are rare where people can actually go to the water and sleep there, and get up in the morning with a cup of coffee, and look out over the water."

In the periods between legislative sessions, State Parks legislative liaison Fred Romero, lobbyist Jim King, and ourselves had been making efforts to get key legislators and staff up to view Cama Beach to see for themselves what a magnificent public resource it was. Over the ensuing years, as legislators changed committee assignments and staffers came and went, Romero, especially, would personally make many such trips to show off Cama. "The eagle would scream out on cue," he says. "People are very impressed with the geography, with the beach. And with the tremendous amount of history that's still there, in relatively good shape. The venue speaks for itself. When they go down to the beach there's sort of an 'ooh' factor that takes over."

To our disappointment the budget proposed for the 2004 legislative session by Governor Locke again did not include additional funding for Cama. In that year the Legislature would be considering a supplemental budget only, and the session would be short. Those of us involved in the lobbying efforts realized we had little time to convince the Legislature of the additional needs, which were substantial due to inflation, redesign work resulting from archaeological impacts, and the complexities of the remaining rehabilitation and new construction work.

The request in outright capital appropriations was $5.4 million, including $1 million for the Commons/Bath House, as the family donations were no longer sufficient due to increased costs as a result of the delays and a more complicated design. The remainder would be for the Boathouse renovation and supporting facilities on the higher elevations. An additional $4.8 million was requested in the form of certificates of participation (COPs) for the new Retreat Lodge and renovation of the cabins, all of which would need to be repaid, with interest, from the revenues from those facilities.

It helped that at long last, major progress had been made on construction. We were able to show legislators photos of Phase 1 work that had actually been accomplished. Additionally, the *Business Plan* became available in February, and we and lobbyist Jim King found the plan to be highly helpful, both in showing the seriousness of the planning efforts for the park, and in depicting a forecast of the likely revenues to be generated by the room rents and other fees when the park became fully operational.

Also, Park Manager Jeff Wheeler devised an attractive handout titled "The Value of Partnerships at Cama Beach State Park." The page detailed the impressive dollar value of all the volunteer hours that had been donated on behalf of Cama Beach, as well as the family's land and cash donations.

During the course of the session, members of Friends of Camano Island Parks and of the Center for Wooden Boats made phone calls and sent emails and letters to legislators. Representative Hans Dunshee, as Chair of the House Capital Budget Committee, had been instrumental in inserting the funding in the House budget bill, and he stood firm on keeping it there. Vice-Chairman Representative Sam Hunt of Olympia and Representatives Barry Sehlin and Barbara Bailey, both of Oak Harbor, also helped.

Although in the minority party at the time, Senator Mary Margaret Haugen was key in insisting that the funding be in any Senate budget. She was backed by Senator Darlene Fairley, Ranking Minority Member on Senate Capital Budget Committee, as well as by Senator Harriet Spanel of Bellingham, Chair of the Democratic Caucus and a long term Cama supporter. Lobbyist Jim King worked hard to convince other key Senators to include the appropriation. The team's accomplishment is especially impressive in that they obtained the willing cooperation of Senator Mike Hewitt of Walla Walla, Chair of the Senate Capital Budget Committee, and of the opposite party. Although the Legislature did not fund the entire amount of the request, when the session ended in early March, significant additional capital funding was in fact

The Value of Partnerships at Cama Beach State Park

Cama Beach State Park Partnerships	Labor Hours	Value of Labor	Value of Materials	Total Value of Donation
Hamalainens & Worthingtons	2,250	$24,750	$12,324,222 *	$12,348,972
Center for Wooden Boats	3,000	$33,000	$100,000 **	$133,000
Americorps, Everett Branch	500	$5,500		$5,500
Artifact Collections Volunteers	300	$3,300		$3,300
Beach Watchers, Island County / WA State University	600	$6,600	$22,500	$29,100
Camano Island Quilters	700	$7,700	$6,000	$13,600
Camp Hosts	5,040	$55,440		$55,440
Friends of Camano Island Parks	30,000	$330,000	$19,000	$349,000
Furniture Builders	2,000	$22,000	$18,000	$40,000
Maintenance Volunteers	2,500	$27,500		$27,500
Office Volunteers	1,000	$11,000		$11,000
Stanwood/Camano Historical Society	500	$5,500		$5,500
Swinomish Tribal Community	Have offered to build a Native American Interpretive Center			Unknown
Tulalip Tribes	Have offered to build a Native American Long House and Dug-out Canoe			Unknown
University of Washington	Weather Station connected to Web Site			$1,500
Total Donations as of December 2003	48,390 hours	$532,290 in labor	$12,489,722 in materials	$13,022,412 total value

* Includes land donations appraised at $9,679,222; design and construction of Commons/Dining Hall and Bath House at $2,235,000; Master Plan at $130,000; legal work at $30,000; and cash donations of $250,000 to date.

** CWB has raised over $100,000 the past 9 months and is working to raise a total of $307,000 for the restoration and improvements of the Boat House.

rev. gw 1/30/04

allocated to the park: $2 million in capital appropriations, and the entire $4.8 million in COPs.

Tribal Concerns Continue

During additional archaeological excavations, two Native American burials were found. The remains were reburied by tribal representatives. In April 2005 the chairman of the Tulalip Tribes wrote a letter to Jeanne Wahler objecting to further excavation work at Cama Beach. The letter said in part, "Given what we now know about the site, we cannot see how a resort, no matter how carefully planned and executed, can be consistent with the site of a tribal burial ground and village." The Tulalip Board of Directors requested a meeting with Ms. Wahler and with the Parks Director and other involved state officials.

It should probably be noted that to date no actual evidence of a mass burial ground, or of a permanent village, has been found. According to archaeologists, the burials appear more likely to have been random, and the site was most likely a seasonal camping area. There is also no evidence that the ancestors of any one tribe were dominant in using the spot; rather, it was likely used at various times by a number of area tribes.

It had been hoped that the park could at last be opened in May 2006, but due to the tribal concerns, plans for further work were again halted for the time being, making meeting that date increasingly unlikely.

In April 2005, on behalf of the family, I drafted and sent a letter to Chairman Jones of the Tulalip Tribes, expressing our interest in becoming better acquainted with tribal leaders and exploring with them the possibilities of how the park could be designed to protect the sanctity of ancestral burials, but yet have portions of the area open to the public. We also said, "We continue to feel it is important that others experience the special atmosphere of this unique place, as well as learn about its history over so many thousands of years." We requested the opportunity to meet with the appropriate tribal representatives in the near future.

The three family members did in fact meet with the Board of Directors of the Tulalip Tribes in their council chamber in May 2005 in what we felt was a cordial exchange of views. It was clear, though, that several of the Board members still had extremely serious concerns regarding burials on the property. A couple of senior members expressed doubts that construction activity could be compatible with the presence of the grave sites. There was a belief among at least two Board members that it was likely that many more bodies were present that had not yet been uncovered, and that the only way to be sure not to desecrate the graves was for the project not to move ahead. Later that same day, the Tulalip Board hosted a meeting with Parks Director Derr, Assistant Director Larry Fairleigh, and Capital Project Manager Mike Allen. Senior tribal leaders again expressed strongly held opinions that a park available for use by the public was incompatible with what was perceived to be an ancestral burial ground. However, some of the tribal Board had not yet visited Cama Beach, and a tour was scheduled for later in the month.

On June 6, 2005, tribal representatives toured the site with State Parks staff, Commissioners, and family members, and were given an overview of the findings of the archaeologists. At that time, around 85 percent of the total construction footprint had been excavated, and open trenches stretched most of the length of the main resort area. A preliminary written summary of the findings by archaeologist Randall Schalk said that in general, the site is a large "late prehistoric shell midden that appears to have been a seasonal fishing and shellfish collecting camp." The camp "was occupied for at least 1,500 years between 300 and 1800 years ago." The report summarized the shellfish and animal bone remains, as well as the woodworking tools, that had been found to date, and stated:

Sandra Worthington examines excavations by Cascadia Archaeology in locations of planned utility trenches, May 2005.

> [The four human burials were] not in an area that was designated for exclusive use as a cemetery. Rather, they are surrounded by and covered over with as much as a meter (3.3 ft) or more of residential refuse (i.e., shellfish remains, bones of fish, mammal, and birds, ash, cooking stones). Native people lived on and carried out routine food processing and waste disposal activities *across all areas of the site—* including the surfaces into which the burials were interred.

State Parks Project Manager Jeanne Wahler emphasized the measures that had been taken to redesign the park for minimal impact, and for the first time publicly mentioned the likelihood that the proposed new Commons/Dining building would be relocated due to the extreme difficulty of engineering a foundation system that would not have significant impacts on the underlying archaeological deposits.

On June 22, in a move publicized in local newspapers, the Tulalip Tribes Board of Directors sent a letter to Parks Director Derr stating the tribe's wish to purchase the park land in order to protect the cultural significance of the site. Senator Haugen expressed how disappointed she and the community would be if the development were halted. Representative Dunshee said he felt the issues could be worked out, and that it was possible both to protect the cultural site and to still have a park available to the people of the state. Director Derr promptly stated that selling Cama Beach to

the Tulalip Tribes was not an option, but he pledged continuing efforts to talk about how the development plans could be modified to accommodate tribal concerns.

In early July 2005, another meeting was held between park officials and the Tulalips. Representatives of the Tulalip, Swinomish, Samish and Upper Skagit tribes also visited Cama again and discussed how to deal with the human remains and how development work might move forward.

The following week, the Tulalips met with State Parks staff on site for additional discussions. That meeting was followed by another involving leaders from the Swinomish, the Upper Skagit, and the Samish. The representatives reiterated that their ancestors also used the Cama Beach area and that their tribes must continue to be included in the discussions.

At the beginning of August, Native American spiritual leaders from the Swinomish and Upper Skagit tribes held a ceremony at Cama Beach to communicate with the spirits of the ancestors whose graves had been disturbed and to lay those spirits to rest. The spiritual elders reported that the ancestral spirits wished to remain in place and not be relocated. And although the spirits did not want additional direct disturbances by further excavations, they were supportive in general of a park, primarily because the site had been a gathering place for so many centuries, as well as a place for layovers on journeys and for exchanges of information. The ancestors reportedly liked the idea of children playing on the beach, and there was no objection to the routing of utility pipes nearby, but the existing trenches should be refilled as soon as possible.

Around this time the Samish decided to withdraw as an affected tribe. The Upper Skagit remained interested, as did the Swinomish, who stated in a letter that they were the successors to the Kikialos tribes who had used the site in earlier centuries. The Tulalips continued to assert their own rights, stating in a letter from Hank Gobin and Richard Young, among other matters, that the site was a significant burial ground with its size and extent still unknown. They again objected to the continuation of park development work.

Meanwhile, the time period in the permit for the archaeological exploration by Cascadia was nearing an end, and the agency applied for a thirty day extension from the Department of Archaeology and Historic Preservation to complete the work originally envisioned. The costs of the archaeological work were now approaching the stunning figure of $2 million dollars, money that had originally been earmarked for construction. Although the Tulalips were asking for yet more archaeological investigation, the consensus within the State Parks agency was that the likelihood of obtaining further significant information was outweighed by the disadvantages of yet more expense, more disturbance of the site, and further delays in the development work.

The Projected Park Opening Date, and Design Changes

At this time, it appeared feasible to work toward opening the park to the public around May 18, 2006; the date was chosen as an anniversary of the original opening of Cama Beach Resort on May 19, 1934. However, the Retreat Lodge and Commons/Dining Building could not be completed by then, and the consensus of the Advisory Committee at its September 2005 meeting was that it would be better not to open the park officially until those major buildings were done. May 2007 would be a more feasible date for the grand opening.

Curt Warber of Parametrix led a discussion which reached a consensus that the proposed Commons Building and Bath House definitely needed to be relocated due to archaeological impacts, with the most suitable site for the new Dining Hall being adjacent to the Retreat Lodge. The Ping Pong room would be remodeled inside for conversion to the restroom/shower building to serve the waterfront cabins and the beach area. Of the remaining bungalows at the northern section of the park, only two, Bungalows A and H, would be retained, with H being moved adjacent to A on the site formerly occupied by B. The boardwalk down the hillside would be eliminated, as it no longer appeared necessary, particularly with the Dining Hall to be located above.

A Further Appeal

The agency received a permit extension from the state Department of Archaeology and Historic Preservation (DAHP) for completing the original scope of the archaeological investigation. In early January 2006, the Tulalip Tribes filed suit in Thurston County Superior Court to appeal the extension of the permit.

The court did not issue a stay of the work, so the final archaeological explorations continued to the extent feasible, given winter weather conditions and the difficulties of water intrusion from high tides. However, the work was drawing to a close. As the utility trenches were refilled, they were lined with a geotextile fabric, so it would be clear in any later excavations where the soil was already disturbed and sifted for artifacts. Numerous bags of materials were taken off-site for further laboratory analysis by Cascadia Archaeology.

Because of the lawsuit, meetings between the tribe and the agency were now limited to talks between the attorneys for each side. In February, representatives from three tribes were present when the graves that had been discovered earlier were filled, and a spirit ceremony was held.

In March, the Superior Court Judge formally denied the appeal of the extension of the permit. At a meeting in Tacoma between State Parks and the Tulalip leadership, a number of issues were discussed. Parks provided the Tulalips with a draft landscaping plan to protect sites where human remains had been found. The Tulalips proposed building the long house interpretive center, originally envisioned in the 2002 settlement agreement, in the area of the bungalows at the north end of the resort area.

In September 2006, the Advisory Committee recommended that the long house be constructed instead in an upland location. In a letter to the Tulalips dated October 5, 2006, Parks Director Derr stated the need to discuss other locations for the long house, suggesting that an upland area might have "significant advantages in terms of proximity to parking, accessibility to the public, and the initial delivery of the bigger story that we want to tell at the park." He stated that after reviewing the ideas with the staff and the families, "We are unwilling to construct a significant new building on the beach." The letter went on to say that such a development would be inconsistent with the Tulalips' longstanding stated preference to reduce development impacts on the beach area and to provide a higher level of protection to the cultural elements in the northern area, and the need to maintain the historic landscape and retain the two remaining bungalows. He emphasized a desire to discuss other means of interpreting the Native American story at the beach.

In November 2006, Tulalip Tribes Chairman Stanley Jones Sr. sent a five page letter to Parks Director Derr responding to Parks' "Draft Cultural Feature Protection Plan" requesting specific additional measures, including larger buffers for the protection of Native American cultural features. Director Derr responded item by item in a letter dated January 2, 2007. In general, the gist of the response was that the measures already planned, plus the modifications to the park design already made, sufficiently increased the level of cultural protection at the site. Parks did agree to increase buffers around sensitive areas by up to 25 feet where feasible, and to a request to place a monument honoring tribal ancestors in a "North Protection Area" at the northern end of the waterfront resort area.

Construction and Renovation in Phase 2B, 2006-2008

Architect Mark Van Vliet, who oversaw the Phase 2B construction work for Parametrix, loves the outdoors and has used parks his entire life. He had worked for four summers at a camp similar to Cama Beach, and he considers his efforts on the Cama project as "a way of giving back." In addition to design work for rehabilitating the historic resort, Van Vliet designed the new Welcome Center, Drop-off Shelter, and Parking Area Restrooms, as well as smaller ancillary structures such as the information kiosks. Van Vliet says that Island County officials were highly cooperative during the process of obtaining permits; in fact, Island County is the easiest jurisdiction he has worked with.

At the end of August 2006, the contract for the Phase 2B development work was awarded to Advanced Construction, Inc., of Mukilteo, owned by A.J. Smith. With the upcoming development work on the waterfront area, the parks staff undertook the huge job of clearing out everything moveable from the resort area buildings. The majority of the items were stored in steel shipping containers in one of the upper parking lots, adjacent to a temporary shelter for the many wooden boats. Karen

Hamalainen helped in sorting out some higher value items to be stored in a more climate-controlled shipping container at Camano Island State Park.

Northwest Region Parks Planner Derek Gustafson, who has a landscape architecture background, was consulted on a multitude of details during the final construction stage. "I'm called out a lot at the last second," he says, "for a lot of little things."

The Waterfront Area Buildings. Because the old resort buildings are on the National Historic Register, the Secretary of the Interior's Guidelines for the Treatment of Historic Properties were adhered to. Of the four treatment options in the guidelines, "rehabilitation" was the one most used. The period of the 1940s was adopted as the period of historic significance for the resort buildings so additions to those structures after 1949 were sometimes removed if they did not appear to add to the historic character.

One of the challenges for architect Van Vliet was that although superficially the waterfront cabins appear identical, each cabin was slightly different from the others in various ways, including the location and extent of the deterioration to be repaired.

Stewardship class at Cama Beach for rangers, 2008. At left is Jeff Wheeler, Cama Beach Park Manager. Facing camera at right is long term Cama staffer Melanie Ford Bissey, Cama Conference Coordinator.

The contractor's prior experience with rehabilitation of historic buildings was limited, so as might be expected, construction of the new buildings in the upper parking areas went smoother than the renovation of the historic resort buildings, where unanticipated difficulties frequently arose. For example, according to Neil McPherson, a supervisor for the contractor, leveling and straightening the former owners' residence planned for offices and meetings took far longer than expected. When the foundation of one section of the house was leveled, the siding would then show gaps, or the interior plaster would crack from being strained into a new position. And so it went, with the leveling of one part throwing another part out of alignment.

The new waterfront area Restrooms/Bathhouse, created in a shell duplicating the old Ping Pong Pen building in the waterfront area, was designed, permitted, and constructed extremely quickly, with the aim of having it completed before the park opening in June 2008.

Van Vliet kept detailed documentation for each building listing the precise repairs made and took photos before, during construction, and after completion.

Resort Area Landscaping. Mark Van Vliet says that raising the level of the area of the waterfront cabins and average of one-and-a-half feet by means of a couple hundred truckloads of fill went smoother than expected. Landscape architect Curt Warber says he was concerned that there might be some "tricky edge spots," where it was necessary to blend the fill into the unfilled areas. He and the Parametrix team had done some early simulations to try to anticipate the finished appearance. He says after the job was done, "I was very relieved when the area felt like it did before." Family members had been apprehensive about the change, but they were also pleased with the result. Sandra Worthington says, "It looks the same—only at the boathouse rear door is the height change apparent."

Landscape architect Jens Swenson mentions the efforts taken to match the new grass seed in the lawn areas to the grass that had been there previously. "The old grass was likely a climax species, self-selected over a period of years to be most suitable to the site. We worked with a seed company to try to replant with the same varieties."

Plants chosen for the beds in front of the former residence include heather, lavender, vinca, and daphne. By the bungalows, it was decided not to replace the original juniper due to maintenance concerns. Instead, flowering hebe was used, as well as ferns and Japanese iris.

The bushes surrounding the small historic children's play area had been damaged during archaeological work and construction. Swenson made efforts to replant with the snowberry bushes and the same variety of wild roses that was there previously. So for color accents, there will again be the white berries and the red rose hips. The lilacs and the ocean spray that were there previously will be encouraged to grow again.

Skilled finish carpenter Craig Quijano worked for contractor Advanced Construction, Inc. on the fine wood craftsmanship in the Welcome Station and other structures. Later he helped supervise the final details on the Phase 2B construction.

The New Parking Area Buildings. Architect Mark Van Vliet strove to make the new Welcome Center, Drop-off Shelter, and Parking Area Restrooms relate well to the old resort structures. The design elements therefore included attention to the building proportions, the vertical siding above horizontal skirting, and details such as the rafter tails, the exposed wood columns inside and out, the stonework column bases on the exterior, and the use of cedar paneling. He also aimed to tie the buildings well into the landscape.

Great efforts were made to use as many sustainable materials as possible, and Van Vliet emphasized that almost all materials for the project were sourced from within Washington State. The cedar paneling in the new buildings, for example, came from Oso Lumber.

The Entry Sign, and the New Small Upper Area Structures. The main park entry sign was designed primarily by Mark Van Vliet and NW Region Parks Planner Derek Gustafson. The wood portion of the sign is a standard type for state parks. The stonework base is similar to others in the park system but customized to be reminiscent of the stone walls at the resort. Considerable effort was put into the location of the sign. It is located to be seen after drivers turn into the park, when they aren't so rushed, so as to give visitors a sense of arrival. The grade for the base was built up so as to make the sign more visible.

The parking area sign kiosks and the small shuttle shelters built in 2007 were designed to be in the same character as the older Cama Beach buildings. Landscape architect Curt Warber says he's pleased with the result: "They're good ornaments, and the park looks like a cultural place as well as a nature facility."

Upper Area Phase 2B Landscaping. The stonework walls at the edge of the hill by the drop-off shelter and restrooms were designed to be reminiscent of the older stone walls in the historic resort area. However, due to safety requirements the new walls had to be built higher than the old, so Parametrix landscape architects Curt Warber and Jens Swenson designed them to be partly "transparent," with a gap between the rock at the bottom and the log rails at the top, similar to the old CCC-era walls built at some other parks. Also, says Warber, "It should be obvious the new structures are not part of the historic fabric that existed before, but they should be part of the same family." The actual masonry work, including the low rock walls at the Welcome Center, was done by Wayne Gagnon of the Marysville area.

1990-91   Park Progress Timeline   **2007** (2008 Opening)

The 2007 Legislative Session

All legislative sessions have had their moments of anguish for those of us involved in lobbying for Cama Beach funds. The 2007 session was in a year of a large revenue surplus and Governor Gregoire came out with the most generous budget in decades for parks and recreation.

Except, inexplicably, for Cama Beach. We were thankful once again for Representative Hans Dunshee, then Vice-Chair of House Appropriations, who inserted funds in the House budget for Cama Beach operating impacts: hiring the necessary additional staff, furnishing the buildings, buying the needed additional equipment and supplies, and operating the park to the end of the biennium.

It helped in justifying the amounts that in the previous year State Parks had hired Ilene Frisch as Budget Director. She acquired an excellent understanding of how the various pieces of the funding request fit together and could back up the figures with solid background information.

The challenge was now to get the capital funds needed to complete some key facilities. In mid-March, the House Capital Budget Committee held a hearing on the proposed budget. In addition to Dick Wagner and Betsy Davis from CWB, several Cama Beach supporters came from Camano to show support, including Peg Hayes Tipton (an active volunteer with the parks, and later a park aide assigned to Camano Island State Park), her mother, and Gerry and Lynn Galloway.

To our frustration, the needed new capital money was not included in the House version of the budget, despite all the efforts by supporters. However, those in the know expected that the funds would be in the Senate version of the budget when it came out, due in no small part to Sen. Haugen's influence.

We were dismayed again when the money also wasn't in the initial Senate budget. As it turned out, there was a mistaken assumption on the part of legislators and their staff that a *re*-appropriation of money that was already committed, but had not yet been spent, was the new appropriation requested in this session. Lobbyist Jim King, the State Parks headquarters staff, and I worked with Senator Haugen and others to clear the matter up. It was a huge relief to finally receive word that some funds been added to the Senate budget. This, when combined with COPs, would pay for the new Retreat Lodge. Also, it was gratifying that funds were appropriated by the Legislature to compensate for those spent on archaeological work, money that had originally been intended for construction. Regrettably, the funding requested for ranger housing, maintenance buildings, and offices did not get included in that session's budget. But at least the two key new buildings, the Retreat Lodge and the Dining Hall (funded by family donations) could now be built.

Reflections on the Long Term Legislative Efforts. Jim King, who has volunteered so much of his professional lobbying skills on behalf of Cama Beach over the years, as well as on parks and recreation issues in general, speaks of the long term efforts toward funding the park: "There was a run of good feelings about Cama Beach. Some of the legislators and staff had gone there as children, so they were familiar with it, and they felt the park was a great thing to do." He says of the later years, "Once the project got going, there was a real desire to get it finished. So much had been put into it, the state had to complete it." Other legislators helped, too, but King says, "The park has such a great champion in Mary Margaret Haugen. She's so well respected, and she carried a lot of the others."

King says that the community partnerships involved with Cama Beach were highly important. "It helped that so many private individuals were involved. By showing the dollar value of the volunteer work and the donations, I could argue that in the big picture the state actually put in a minority of the funding."

He emphasizes: "It was not a case of a group coming down to Olympia and saying, 'Do this for us!' It's always better when people say, "We're putting a lot in ourselves, and we'd like some help with it."

Mary Margaret Haugen is consistently credited with being Cama Beach's best known advocate in the Legislature. But she also mentions other State Senators who were of particular help to the Cama project over the years: Dan McDonald from Bellevue, Karen Fraser from Olympia, and Harriet Spanel from Bellingham. On the House side, she particularly cites Representatives Barry Sehlin, Dave Anderson, and Hans Dunshee.

Some Events and Activities, 2006-2008

Eric Watilo, Cama Beach's Regional Supervisor. In early 2006, experienced senior ranger Eric Watilo became the direct supervisor of the manager of Cama Beach State Park. As Assistant Northwest Region Manager, Watilo reviewed the various operational plans for Cama Beach. Among his many other duties, he assumed responsibility for finalizing the agreement between State Parks and The Center for Wooden Boats, as well as the pending agreement with the Beach Watchers for their activities at Cama.

Storm Damage. November 2006 was a month of wind and rain storms, making construction work difficult. A number of trees were lost to winds in the Cama parking lots. Three CWB boats were heavily damaged by falling trees or limbs, and some of the metal storage containers in the parking lots were dented. FOCIP volunteers put in over a hundred hours of clean up work in that month alone.

The Center for Wooden Boats Agreement. As the contractor worked on the waterfront area renovations at Cama Beach, The Center for Wooden Boats held another annual Mothers' Day Sail off the beach at Camano Island State Park in 2006 with 180 to 200 people attending, many of them going for sails on the *Adventuress*. Sold for the first time were CWB caps and T-shirts bearing a logo with the Cama Beach cabins and a CWB sailboat and bearing the wording "The Center for Wooden

Signing of the partnership agreement on March 1, 2008, between The Center for Wooden Boats and Washington State Parks for CWB's Cama Beach campus. In foreground, left to right: CWB Founding Director Dick Wagner; State Parks Commissioner Bob Petersen (slightly behind); Parks Director Rex Derr; CWB Board President David Loretta (signing). CWB Executive Director Betsy Davis at far right.

Boats at Cama Beach State Park." An equally successful sailing event was held on Mother's Day in 2007.

The thirty-year partnership agreement between The Center for Wooden Boats and State Parks covering its operations at Cama Beach is complex, with many details worked out over a period of at least ten years. CWB Founding Director Dick Wagner now says, "There were good reasons for the delays," given the complicated issues involved.

The agreement was signed, at last, on March 1, 2008, in Seattle at CWB's annual fundraising auction event. CWB took over use of Cama Beach's Boathouse, the former Fire Truck Garage (now classroom space), the Workshop, and the Boatman's House. It also has rights to use three deluxe cabins for housing its instructors and staff.

The Expanded Advisory Committee. A continuing minor concern in recent years had been providing a more formal status for the Advisory Committee that had been meeting since 1998. In October 2006, Director Rex Derr signed the charter formally establishing the Cama Beach State Park Advisory Committee. I was elected interim chairperson and Betsy Davis of CWB as vice-chair. The newly chartered committee be-

Discussion of food catering plans for the new park. Left to right: Tom Oliva, State Parks Enterprise Coordinator; Sandra Worthington, a former Cama Beach owner who helped solicit vendors; Jeff Wheeler, Cama Beach Area Manager.

gan officially meeting in early 2007 with an expanded membership of community representation.

In addition to the family and CWB stalwarts, regular attendees now also included Carol Triplett and Tom Eisenberg representing FOCIP; Scott Chase representing Beach Watchers; Lawrence Baum of Camano Sail representing the Camano Island Chamber of Commerce; and Candy Trautman and Karen Prasse representing the Stanwood Area Historical Society. Representatives from all interested Native American tribes were formally invited from the beginning, though actual involvement was gradual, with Stillaguamish chairman Shawn Yanity and that tribe's cultural resource staff being the first. Additional CWB representatives began attending, including board member Walt Plimpton and volunteer contractor Brian Greene; and Josh Flickner also came on behalf of the Chamber of Commerce.

Gordon Bell, ranger at Cama Beach State Park.

New Park Staff is Hired

In December 2007, Gordon Bell joined Cama Beach as an additional ranger after experience at other parks and an earlier landscaping career. His wife Debra quickly became an active volunteer with the park and later became part of the staff.

Among the many other volunteers over the years, Alice Blandin, with her valuable office skills, was one of the longest serving, and she was at last employed full time in 2008.

Preparing for the Opening. In the Northwest Region office, Allison Alderman began refreshing the operating budget request in 2008 in anticipation of the additional funding needed for opening and staffing the Retreat Lodge and Dining Hall after their completion. "I'm really, really excited," she says, "that we actually have roads and other facilities now, that progress is being made by the contractors."

Alice Blandin, long term volunteer, and office staff. *(Photo by Tina Dinzl-Pederson, Cama Beach State Park)*

Tom Riggs, ranger at Camano Island State Park, explored the various types of electric and hybrid vehicles available and recommended the final selections which were purchased.

Jim Farmer, former manager at Fort Worden State Park, assisted in getting the reservation system and communications equipment operational. Because high speed internet was not available on Camano Island, a microwave link with Whidbey Island was installed. Farmer says that Cama Beach is now the most advanced technologically of any state park, due especially to the centralized monitoring and control systems, including fire alarms, building heating, water supply, and sewage pumping.

Sandra Worthington took on the task of lining up caterers to provide meals for persons staying at Cama during the interim before the Dining Hall opens. She also began helping plan furnishings for the Retreat Lodge and Dining Hall.

Karen Hamalainen worked with park staff to prioritize the relative historical importance of the many items from the resort that are now in the care of State Parks, and to help select items that are appropriate for interpretive exhibits.

FOCIP work party on Cranberry Lake Trail, 2008. Pictured: Jerry Nielsen (foreground); Carol Triplett. *(Photo by Tina Dinzl-Pederson Cama Beach State Park)*

Ranger Gordon Bell discusses park flower bed plantings with Sandra Worthington, former Cama Beach owner, April 2008.

The Cama Beach Quilters began sewing new curtains for the cabins. FOCIP volunteers completed the trail along the bluff near the parking area as well as improving the trail to Cranberry Lake.

The Educational and Interpretive Programs

In January 2008, Christina "Tina" Dinzl-Pederson was selected from a talented pool of applicants for the important position as Parks Interpretive Specialist to develop Cama's programs and exhibits for the public. As an organizing scheme for the educational offerings, she soon came to see the different interpretive program components as spokes on a wheel radiating out from the hub of the site's geologic and natural history: the Native American use, the loggers who cleared the old growth, the vacationers playing on the waterfront during the resort period, the marine life, the upland plants and animals.

"I love my job," she says. "I'm excited on a personal level. This type of education is timely." She cites the recent book, *Last Child in the Woods: Saving Our Children from Nature-Deficit Disorder*, by Richard Louv, saying, "It's important to get children out in nature, to get people more reconnected with their environment, in contact with little critters, with the weather, with plants." It's essential for "heathier bodies, but also to educate

Tina Dinzl-Pederson, Cama Beach State Park Interpretive Specialist, with one of her many puppets for use in children's programs.

people on how the natural environment affects us globally, on a larger scale than just as individuals."

Also, referring to the unique historical aspects of Cama Beach, she says, "It was so important that the family saved the buildings. There's only this one fishing resort remaining out of the many that formerly existed around Puget Sound. People can come and experience things that happened in the past, as well as build for the future."

In addition to the park staff, the Beach Watchers and other volunteers will be major participants in the interpretive programs, acting as docents and assisting in other ways to help enhance the public's experience of Cama Beach.

How Cama Beach State Park is "Green." Major efforts have gone into designing the new park to be as sustainable as possible in both its construction and its operations, given budgetary and practical constraints.

Project Manager Jeanne Wahler points out that the fact that so many older buildings are being reused is an immense saving in environmental costs through not having to dispose of debris from demolished structures or to buy a huge quantity of materials for new buildings.

Some of the many other environmentally sensitive features of the new park include:

• Wherever feasible, the existing resort buildings have been insulated to conserve heat. The heating in all the buildings is controlled by a computerized

1990-91   Park Progress Timeline   **2008 Opening**

central management system that can be programmed to turn down heat in specific structures at times of the day when they are not being used. Sensors detect when buildings are occupied and then turn the heat on if needed.

• The hot water heaters in the buildings are "on demand" systems so it is not necessary to continuously keep the water in tanks heated.

• To the extent feasible, building materials were purchased from local sources to minimize the costs and energy involved in transportation.

• The new Dining Hall/Commons Building will be built to Leadership in Energy and Environmental Design (LEED) silver standards.

• Environmentally benign Marmoleum is used wherever appropriate for surfaces such as floors and countertops.

• Waste material at the park will be minimized and recycled to the maximum extent practical.

• Island Transit will provide free bus service to the park, and visitors are encourage to use that means of transportation.

• Visitors' vehicles are parked away from the waterfront area to minimize noise, congestion, pollution, and fossil fuel use.

One of the "zero emission" electric vehicles at Cama Beach State Park.

• Most vehicles used to shuttle guests to the waterfront area will be electric or hybrid gas-electric powered to minimize emissions and petroleum usage.

• Native plants are used in the landscaping to minimize the use of water and fertilizers.

The Grand Opening in 2008

The official Grand Opening for the park was at last set for Saturday, June 21, 2008. Park Manager Jeff Wheeler would act as master of ceremonies. Native American spiritual leaders would begin and end the event with blessings. As this book went to press, it appeared likely that Governor Christine Gregoire would speak. Also speaking briefly would be former owners Karen Risk Hamalainen and Sandra Risk Worthington, key Cama Beach legislative supporters Senator Mary Margaret Haugen and Representative Hans Dunshee, Parks Commission members, Island County Commissioner John Dean, CWB's Dick Wagner, and Washington State Parks Foundation Executive Director Tom Lattimore.

A replica of the log archway with a "Cama Beach" sign that stood for many years at the bottom of the hill road would be raised to symbolize the historic resort's rebirth. Cabins would again be available for rent. Although it would be more than a year before completion of the new Dining Hall and the Retreat Lodge, the public could again, after the hiatus of so many years, enjoy the unrivaled ambience of the site.

Some Conclusions on the Long Park Process

Agency Director Rex Derr speaks of five important ways that the Cama Beach project is "right on the mark" as the state's first park to open in the 21st century:

First, the family's original concept of "an outdoor education site in the urbanizing Puget Sound region is exactly what's needed at this time." And the fact that the family aimed the project at the state level, rather than as a county park or a national park, was the right approach for funding. "The federal government is more removed from connections with local people, and the county parks are struggling harder financially. The state is better at financing this type of facility."

A unique benefit of Cama Beach is that "the park retains historical compo-nents, as well as natural and cultural amenities. Even though the agency was tested" by the Native American cultural

Rex Derr, Director of State Parks, seated in a rocking chair made by Cama Beach Furniture Makers and holding a quilt by the Cama Beach Quilters, 2008.

aspects, State Parks learned from the experience, and these cultural attributes "add another level of value to what a 'whole service' state park should be."

Importantly, Cama Beach will generate sufficient revenues to be "partly sustainable financially with the ability to grow with its programs. This is in line with State Park trends."

Derr concludes, "The mosaic of partnerships with The Center for Wooden Boats, FOCIP, and hopefully the tribes, will help sustain the park forever, like Fort Worden. It's early in the evolution, and we still have to discover the full potential of the partnerships."

Occasionally someone asks, "If you had known it would take eighteen years to get the park open to the public, would you still have done it?"

The answer, of course, is "Definitely!"

As Diane Lenius of Parametrix says, "There's only one Cama Beach!"

Retiring Parks Northwest Region Manager Terry Doran comments, "I'm excited every time I go there."

Agency Director Rex Derr observes, "The park is a big and beautiful project for us, clearly worth our shifting of staff resources and funds to get the park developed. Cama Beach is an opportunity to do the park right first, rather than change it later— to make sure we do whatever we can in a sustainable, 'green' fashion, to translate and interpret that method of lifestyle to young people. New ways of doing things, new equipment, a model of what we need to do for the rest of the park system. "

What Might Have Been Done Differently

In hindsight, stronger and more persistent efforts should have been made earlier to contact the interested Native American tribes on a formal, government-to-government basis; to undertake more extensive archaeological investigation; and to encourage tribal participation in the planning process. However, State Parks and Recreation Commission member Joan Thomas comments, "I feel we've been patient and tried very hard to do the right thing. We learned a lot and benefitted from the experience. The agency needed to know how to deal with tribes since tribal issues are involved in a number of parks."

Director Derr says that even though considerable effort was spent on tribal issues, "there's so much more that will be gratifying. We have to embrace the future and different ways of working with a subset of society that's growing in influence and respect." Like Commissioner Thomas, he feels the agency can apply what it has learned to its relationships with other tribes, at other parks.

Parks Capital Program Manager Mike Allen points out how dramatically different two cultures can be "even though living elbow-to-elbow. Project managers can't go into a project without being aware they have to collaborate with interested tribes, or they can get stuck in a legal or regulatory rut." He mentions that as a result of state projects encountering Native American burials at other sites, particularly near Port Angeles, Governor Gregoire promulgated an executive order requiring public agencies involved with construction projects to deal with cultural resources up front.

Allen also observes, "The archaeology work for Cama Beach cost around $2.5 million. It's not a nickel and dime issue any more. Before, there was never a line item in a project's budget for archaeology. Now it's a major part of project funding."

Most of us involved in the park's development were also naive about just how complex and how expensive it would be to turn a rustic 1930s seasonal resort into a year round park that would meet modern building codes, Shoreline Management Act regulations, federal marine laws, health and sanitation standards, ADA access, and generally expected levels of comfort. State Parks, as a relatively small state agency, has limited staff resources and often meager funding options. Difficult choices must frequently be made in allocating priorities for capital development work.

As non-agency partners in the project, it seems to family members that the agency tried hard to handle the project well, despite the limited staffing and financial resources and frequent obstacles, and that it mostly succeeded.

The Cama Beach State Park Advisory Committee is an excellent mechanism for updating partners and other interested non-agency persons, as well as for obtaining the benefit of their experience and advice. These other stakeholders might be more consistently consulted on key discussions and changes.

No doubt it was difficult at times for some agency personnel to feel they should set aside other work to devote their attention to a project with many interruptions and with completion dates that kept getting pushed farther into the future. Still, at times the work might have progressed faster if such a large and visible project had more often clearly been made a focused priority for the agency's staff at all levels, at least for limited periods, recognizing that those involved could not always know precisely the next step in such a complex undertaking.

Some Final Reflections from Key Persons in the Project

Sandra Worthington comments on what's been done with her family's heritage, "With the new buildings and facilities, State Parks is giving new life to the original, and I think they've preserved that original feel very well."

Park Manager Jeff Wheeler observes, "Cama Beach is a magical spot. It's been drawing people for thousands of years. It's hard not to *feel* that as you go down the hill. We didn't need to ask people to volunteer to help at the park. They come there and they sense that magic and they ask to be involved." He considers State Parks and himself as merely "caretakers of the land. Nobody really 'owns' the land. It was there before all of us, and it will be there after us.

"Cama Beach is unique," Wheeler adds, "as a park built around a mission statement, and around environmental education." He sees Cama as "a leader for parks that come in the future."

Regarding the major land donations, he observes, "Cama Beach carries on a tradition of giving to the state park system that started with Mr. Moran, who donated Moran State Park" in 1921.

Parametrix Project Manager Damon McAlister talks of the collaborative effort of the large design and engineering team, which had virtually all conceivable specialties involved. "It's been a real unique project that way." Despite the roadblocks and hurdles, "Everyone bought into the vision and feels invested in the project. There was a lot of additional effort, going above and beyond what was expected." He particularly mentions Jeanne Wahler for keeping everyone focused on the wider vision for the project. He praises Mark Van Vliet for tenacity over such an extended period in keeping building costs in check, construction moving, and achieving a high quality result, despite difficult weather conditions and frequent frustrations.

Hopefully all who experience Cama Beach will feel that whatever the ups and downs of the long creation of the park, the resulting unique ambience proves that it was all worthwhile. As Planning Manager Bill Koss notes, "If visitors say, 'I'm changed for having been there,' or if old-timers say it's like reliving the '50s, '60s, or '70s, we will have been successful."

Melanie Ford Bissey, Cama Beach Conference Coordinator. *(Photo by Tina Dinzl-Pederson, Cama Beach State Park)*

Long term Cama staffer and Conference Coordinator Melanie Ford Bissey, whose position includes marketing and promotion for the park, comments: "I don't feel like I'm 'selling' Cama to the public— I'm offering people a real benefit. I believe in Cama Beach. I love getting people outdoors, enjoying the environment, into boats, up to Cranberry Lake, caring about the planet. In the larger picture, the mission of State Parks is very important."

Dick Wagner, Founding Director of The Center for Wooden Boats, sees the park as "adding new dimensions to partnerships between state government and a nonprofit organization. I feel proud of leading a new way to design parks. Cama Beach will be considered a landmark in park planning."

CWB Executive Director Betsy Davis speaks of how Cama Beach fits in with all of her organization's core values: "Building community between people of all ages; promoting stewardship of the place, of people, of boats, and of craftsmanship; and providing affordable access to the water for everyone, as well as hands-on experiences."

Jeanne Wahler, Project Manager of Cama Beach for the agency says, "Once someone's been to see Cama, there's no doubt in their mind that it needs to be protected

Jeanne Wahler (left), State Parks' Project Manager for Cama Beach, speaks with State Parks Commissioner Fred Olson (center), and Larry Fairleigh, State Parks AssistantDirector for Resource Development during a tour of the park, April 2008. In the background is an on-demand hot water heater in the new restroom/bath house building.

and enjoyed. It speaks highly for the place that it has that kind of consensus among people from varying points of view. Personally, it was an honor to be involved in something so special. To take something so complex and know it will have a national and international draw."

Parks Capital Project Manager Mike Allen mentions that the project is the largest in terms of dollar amounts that the agency has ever taken on. But "despite having the most complexities and frustration of any project, it's also the most fulfilling. To see what can be done with the old structures and how they can still be made useful for another fifty years or more, it's just amazing."

Retiring Northwest Region Manager Terry Doran says, "I feel proud to have been a part of it. We stayed true to the basic mission and its parameters from day one. We built a unique park around the unique setting." Commissioner Joan Thomas feels the Commission "fulfilled its obligation to be stewards of the past, for the benefit of future generations."

State Representative Hans Dunshee reflects about the Cama Beach funding in the state budget: "It was real, not just words and numbers. It was a unique opportunity to add immensely to the inventory of public beaches. That's the people's waterfront there, and I can say I had a role in helping make it happen. It makes me glad to be able to go there and walk on the beach, or to look out a cabin window and see the orcas go by. It will be a great park. People from all around the country will come."

Senator Mary Margaret Haugen looks back on so many legislative sessions: "We always get to ask for something in the capital budget. Mine was always, 'Cama Beach, Cama Beach, Cama Beach!' It's been so exciting to watch the people in the community taking ownership of it, writing letters to the legislature, volunteering. It's going to be a huge success—the crown jewel of Camano Island, and the crown jewel of the state park system."

Commissioner Bob Petersen feels his participation in the project has been extremely gratifying to him personally: "I'm one of the persons who made it happen. I can look back at it and say I made a difference. It's one of the high points of my life."

Senator Mary Margaret Haugen holds a quilt by the Cama Beach Quilters. From the initial concept of the park through the many years until its opening, Sen. Haugen has been the project's longest term and most vigorous supporter in the Legislature. *(2008 photo, courtesy of Washington State Parks)*

The others of us who were significantly involved in the process feel exactly the same way.

The Author gets the Last Word

In a letter dated June 21, 1993, and published in the *Stanwood/Camano News*, the family detailed its philosophy about the park. In addition to specifically mentioning the anticipated environmental education programs, the youth programs to be offered by The Center for Wooden Boats, and the planned trail network, we said:

"We see Cama Beach as a place where people can go to renew themselves. Cama Beach's unique natural setting will give each of us an opportunity to relax away from the frantic pace of our everyday concerns, to get in touch again with what is truly important in life."

That type of place is needed today even more than when the statement was written fifteen years ago.

I feel extremely fortunate to have had a role in such a significant, worthwhile, enduring project. Turning Cama Beach into a major state park became an important calling for me, contributing immensely to meaning for my life and making my time on earth count for something larger than myself.

If the park is to truly fulfill the dream all of us have had for it, we must all continue to work on its behalf. And as the years pass, additional public spirited persons must devote themselves to the park and make its vision their own.

Having seen the enthusiasm and good will toward Cama Beach from so many people to date, I'm confident its future as a state park with a unique mission will be secure. Generations upon generations will come to this place to enjoy the beauty of the beach and the serenity of the forest; to learn about the natural environment and reconnect with it; to experience the pleasures of wooden boats; to gaze at the splendor of the starry night sky; and to renew themselves spiritually.

And Now, the Park Needs You

All parks have a continuing need for donations of both volunteer time and money. That's why the proceeds from the sale of this book are dedicated to funding Cama Beach.

In general, the future of Cama Beach as a state park is up to *you*, the visitor, and the enthusiastic user and supporter.

Join or become active in the Friends of Camano Island Parks (FOCIP), the Beach Watchers, The Center for Wooden Boats, the Stanwood Area Historical Society, or any of the other groups involved at the park.

Especially in periods when state money is tight, parks may be a tempting target for budget cuts. Our magnificent state park system needs your continuing support. Tell your legislators your opinions about funding.

You can also make monetary donations to Cama Beach, including specific projects, either through the park itself or through the Washington State Parks Foundation at www.WashingtonStateParksFoundation.org.

With respect to Cama Beach, as of this writing:

• More meeting and classroom space is needed.

• A Native American interpretive center would be an important addition, perhaps in the form of a long house, possibly adjacent to the upper parking areas.

• A new park maintenance shop and more office spaces are badly needed, as is on-site ranger housing.

• A highly desirable, but costly, infrastructure improvement is increased generator capacity for backup electrical power during the outages which often occur during windstorms, particularly in the late fall and winter seasons.

An Important Opportunity: The Recreation Hall

A specific project in need of major cash donations is reconstructing the Recreation Hall that burned in 1977. This building was highly important as a center of activities at Cama Beach Resort.

The building would provide meeting, classroom, and exhibit spaces, as well as a small café to serve the waterfront area with food and beverages, and as a casual gathering and conversation space.

The most useful approach is rebuilding the earlier hall's wood frame exterior, with the interior modified to meet current needs. Because the original hall rested on numerous small pads, without excavations for a deep foundation, reconstructing it would not significantly impact the underlying archaeological deposits. Nor should there be major permitting problems, since it would be a reconstruction of an historic building previously on the site. The water, sewer, and electrical lines are already in place, ready to be connected to the building.

If you would like to contribute toward this highly visible and needed project, please contact either the park manager or the Washington State Parks Foundation (www.washingtonstateparksfoundation.org). The tax-deductible donation will be a lasting legacy.

And afterwards, come again to enjoy the gathering spot you helped create.

Recreation Hall (right), from a resort post card.

The Cama Beach State Park icon is available as a colored poster in two sizes through www.parks.wa.gov

APPENDIX 1

Vision Statement

Cama Beach State Park is a large, mostly undisturbed forest with an extensive beachfront on an inside passage in Puget Sound. The park preserves a rich diversity of plants and animals on the beach and tidelands and in the upland forest. The forest extends away from the saltwater to encompass an isolated small lake and wetland area. Located on the west shore of Camano Island, Washington, the park is a secluded, peaceful haven, in sharp contrast to the urban growth in the Puget Sound basin.

Cama Beach State Park offers both a footprint of the past, with its rustic beachfront facilities and the potential for a well directed step into a future that combines contemporary park and educational facilities with its historic landscape. This step serves contemporary public needs and reflects an enduring appreciation for the parks diverse natural and cultural resources.

To achieve this vision, State Parks is guided by these tenets:

• *Development and operation of the park emphasizes stewardship of its land and water resources. Recycling of wastes is demonstrated and practiced.*

• *Development and operation of the park retain the character-defining features of the historic site.*

• *The history of the fishing resort is interpreted and incorporated into the rehabilitation and maintenance of the resort facilities.*

• *The Center for Wooden Boats (CWB), a direct experience maritime museum recreates the historic boat livery at Cama Beach, in which the public can try out traditional wooden boats at affordable rates. CWB also provides instruction in the whole spectrum of maritime heritage skills, from boat building to sailing the old classics. The programs include people who are young and not so young and who have a wide range of abilities.*

• *A preservation plan directs the rehabilitation, protection and/or removal of resort buildings and landscape features consistent with U.S. Department of Interior guidelines.*

• *Ecologically sound land use governs the design and extent of day use and overnight facilities.*

• *Public health, safety, and Americans with Disabilities Act standards guide development of all park facilities.*

• *Day use and overnight facilities meet both local community and state wide needs for access and accommodation.*

• *The park's outstanding educational qualities are available to individuals and groups of varied ages through development of educational and interpretive features, including an environmental learning and conference center and trails.*

• *An environmental learning and conference center, developed to reflect master plan guidelines, is operated by a nonprofit organization, the state, or a combination of both.*

• *Opportunities to enhance revenue and offset capital and maintenance costs are explored and implemented where appropriate to the integrity of the historic property and park vision.*

• *Efforts are made to provide a portion of the park's resources for recreational shellfish harvesting as well as beach combing; remaining marine resources may be considered for a marine preserve.*

• *Private vehicular traffic within the park is minimized. Alternative types of circulation within the park and access to it, which may include marine access facilities, are explored.*

• *Park access and circulation is consistent with the Island County Comprehensive Trails Plan, the Cascadia Marine Trail system and other regional recreational and circulation plans.*
• *Cama Beach State Park provides opportunities for the public that complement opportunities available at Camano Island State Park.*

APPENDIX 2

Those testifying on July 12, 1992, in Anacortes before the State Parks and Recreation Commission in support of acquiring Cama Beach as a state park were:
Washington State Representative Mary Margaret Haugen, Camano Island; Berit Kaae, Island County Planner; Fred E. Ellis, Shaw Island; Eugene "Lefty" K. Wootten, Camano Island; Peggy J. Swendsen, Stanwood; Robert N. Larson, Mayor, City of Stanwood; Richard C. Bergholz, Camano Island; Don Hanna, Camano Island (also presented letters from teachers in support); Richard Schoonover, Camano Island; George D. Wyse, Island County Park and Recreation Board, Camano Island; Dorothy Wakefield Murray, Camano Island; Harvey A. Jansma, Camano Island; Frank M. Strohecker, Vice-President of the Camano Island Homeowners Association, Camano Island; and three family members: Karen Risk Hamalainen, Asko Hamalainen, and Sandra Risk Worthington.

Excerpted from an email from Bill Koss, State Parks Planning Program Manager, August 21, 2002:

"Many people deserve recognition in getting the development of Cama Beach to its current stage. Here is a brief, and no doubt incomplete list:
• Karen Hamalainen and Sandra Worthington, and their spouses Asko and Gary, whose vision and support initiated the acquisition and development
• Cleve Pinnix for supporting this through the budgeting trials and tribulations
• Terry Doran, Allison Alderman, Frank Galloway, Jeff Wheeler, Melanie and Richard: the region and park staff who keep the site alive, deal with the day-to-day matter, the community, adroitly use duct tape and baling wire to hold a historic site together
• Arnie Larsen for bringing engineering skill and patience to the table
• Dick Wager and Richard Kolin from the Center for Wooden Boats, the anchor tenant instrumental in getting the property alive and whose presence will assure daily vigor on the site
• David Herrick who provided an intellectual framework for use in analyzing issues thoughtfully
• Diane Lenius, Neil Bass, Gary Maynard, Curt Warber, et al from Parametrix who prepared blueprints and permitted the project
• Dan Meatte for intellectual and archaeological guidance through trying periods
• Randall Schalk for unflagging efforts in winter archaeology and permitting hell
• Tom Oliva for energizing the Retreat Lodge funding and design
• Barbara Herman for working through a challenging appeal process
• Jim Ellis who is fated to resume his role as planner extraordinaire for the site, a task he started more than a decade ago.

"The list could go on and on. And I'm sure I inadvertently omitted somebody....Many people came to the support of the project in the Legislature, getting $4 million appropriated in a very tight budget period."

Groups included at the June 19, 2004, Active Volunteer Summit at Cama Beach, and the persons speaking for them were (in order of the presentations);

Cama Beach archival project, with Susan Kratochvil speaking;
Backyard Wildlife Habitat, presented by Val Schroeder;
WSU/Island County Beach Watchers, by Scott Chase;
Camp hosts, by William Wallace;
The Center for Wooden Boats, by Dick Wagner and Betsy Davis;
Friends of Camano Island Parks, by Carol Triplett;
Nature programs at Camano Island parks, by Melanie Ford Bissey;
Cama Beach Quilters, by Audrey McEwen;
Stanwood Area Historical Society, by Karen Prasse;
University of Washington, by David Finalyson;
Cama Beach Woodworkers, by Nick Van;
State Parks Northwest Region Resources, by David Newcomb;
Worthington Foundation, by Sandra Worthington;
Hamalainen Charitable Trust, by Karen Hamalainen.

SOURCES

A note regarding the sources:

As this book is not intended as a scholarly document, I have not tried to provide complete citations for every statement. However, since some readers or users may wish to know where information in the text came from, I've tried to mention the main sources for most assertions.

Unless otherwise noted, all documents are from my own files and originated in the actual time period discussed. If no document is cited, the information came from my personal notes of meetings or phone calls, or from the written minutes of the Cama Beach Advisory Committee meetings.

The Centuries of Native American Use

Most details on Native American life are taken from:
(1) Osmundson, John. "Camano Island—Succession of Occupation from Prehistoric to Present Time." *The Washington Archaeologist.* April 1961: 2-18.
(2) Osmundson, John Skinner. *Man and His Natural Environment on Camano Island.* A thesis submitted in partial fulfillment of the requirements for the degree of Master of Arts in Anthropology, Washington State University, 1964.

The information about burials is from information provided by Hank Gobin, Tulalip Cultural Resources Manager, as summarized in an article in the *Herald* (Everett, WA), July 6, 2005.

The archaeological information comes mainly from a report: Schalk, Randall, Renee Schwarzmiller, Stephen Kenady, Charles Hodges, Rebecca Wigen, and Brian Herbel. 2002. *Supplemental Testing at 45IS2, Cama Beach State Park, Camano Island, Washington.* Cascadia Archaeology, Seattle, Washington.

The Logging Years

Information in this section came largely from Karen Prasse's book, and from articles by John Osmundson in the *Stanwood News*, September 12 and 19, 1963.

The Resort Years

Many of the details of the resort construction are taken from an article in the *Stanwood News*, January 28, 1971, by Alice Essex, who relied on Muriel Risk's oral assertions. The reliability of some of the details in the article is open to question, and it is probably impossible at this point to know the degree to which the information is valid. But it is the only known available source for some of the assertions.

How the Resort Operated

Unless otherwise attributed, most information came from the oral reminiscing of Karen Risk Hamalainen and Sandra Risk Worthington, and occasionally from my own memories of the resort.

The Long Path to a State Park

Gov. Lowry visit: Quote is from the *Stanwood/Camano News*, September 5, 1995.

Formation of the Advisory Group: Author's files, particularly his own notes of meetings he attended.

A Sobering Flood: November 29, 1998, email from Hugh Shipman.

The Cama Beach Institute: June 28, 1999, email from Linde DeVere; notes of phone conversations with David Herrick on May 11 and August 18, 1999; an email from David Herrick dated August 5, 1999; a copies of CBI's draft operational plans; a CBI brochure draft; a draft copy by David Herrick of the proposed "Captured by Cama" project; and other materials.

Dining Hall Concerns: December 8, 1999, email from Gerry Tays to Kate Johnson of Leavengood Architects with copies to Bill Koss and Flo Lentz.

Archaeological Explorations and Tribal Concerns: The information about the fourteen month period of the delay is from a "Cama Beach History" time line compiled by State Parks as background information for the Legislature.

Negotiations with tribes re: utility corridors: Email from Bill Koss, May 24, 2001.

Shoreline permit; Tulalip appeal: Emails from Bill Koss, September 11, 2001; November 8, 2001; April 16 and May 7, 2002.

A Transition: Email from Bill Koss, August 21, 2002.

The 2003 Funding Situation: April 16, 2003, email from Larry Fairleigh; April 20, 2003 email from the author.

2005 negotiations with the tribes:
Herald (Everett, WA), June 23, 2005; June 24, 2005; July 9, 2005; July 14, 2005; July 16, 2005.

Author's notes from a conversation with Jeanne Wahler August 8, 2005, and from the Cama Advisory Group meeting August 8, 2005.

Another Tulalip Appeal: Advisory Group notes from January 9, 2006.

2006-7 Tribal negotiations:
Letters: Tulalip Chairman Jones to Parks Director Derr, November 3, 2006; Parks Director Derr to Tulalip Chairman Jones, October 5, 2006, and January 2, 2007.

ACKNOWLEDGMENTS

I am indebted to the following for help with this book:

For Photographs, Illustrations, and Background Materials:
Karen Prasse, Bill Blandin, and the Stanwood Area Historical Society
Dave Pinkham, Stanwood/Camano NEWS
Randall Schalk and Michael Wolverton, Cascadia Archaeology
Dan Meatte, Archaeologist, State Parks
Carol Triplett, Friends of Camano Island Parks
Melanie Ford Bissey and Tina Dinzl-Pederson, Cama Beach State Park

The Persons Interviewed (in alphabetical order):

State Legislators
Representative Hans Dunshee
Senator Mary Margaret Haugen

The Washington State Parks and Recreation Commission
Commissioner Bob Petersen
Commissioner Joan Thomas
Director Rex Derr
Director Cleve Pinnix (retired)

The Management and Staff, Washington State Parks
Allison Alderman
Mike Allen
Tina Dinzl-Pederson
Terry Doran
Jim Ellis (retired)
Larry Fairleigh
Dick Fankhauser (retired)
Melanie Ford Bissey
Derek Gustafson
Bill Koss
Fred Romero
Jeanne Wahler
Jeff Wheeler

Parametrix
Diane Lenius
Damon McAlister
Jens Swenson
Mark Van Vliet
Curt Warber

Atelier
Janis Snoey (former principal)

Cascadia Archaeology
Randall Schalk

The Center for Wooden Boats
Dick Wagner
Betsy Davis
Rich Kolin

Volunteers
David Herrick (formerly Cama Beach Institute)
Carol Triplett (FOCIP)
Jim King (Citizens for Parks and Recreation)
Don Meehan (for WSU Extension/Island County Beach Watchers)

Former Guests at Cama Beach Resort:
Barbara Cook
Tom Cook
Melanie Cook-Hartley
Judy Beeman Graham
Chapin Krafft
Laura Strance Poston

Community Members:
Nels Bodin
Ole Eide (Transcription of oral interview)

The Family:
Karen Hamalainen
Asko Hamalainen
Sandra Worthington
Gary Worthington

Proofreaders (alphabetical order):
Linda Crabtree, Evelyn Greenberg, Carol Horner, Emily Ray, Deb Ross, Pete Taylor, Ginny Taylor, Mary Anne Trause, Paul Trause, Ruth Weber, Linda Whitcher, Sandra Worthington

About the Author

Gary Worthington grew up in Stanwood. He often visited future wife Sandra Risk at her family's Cama Beach Resort when the couple dated in high school. He fondly remembers riding with Sandra in the *Cama Princess II* down the marine railway while her father operated the electric cable winch, as well as rowing and swimming off the beach on warm summer days.

Gary also has good memories of being a park aide at Camano Island State Park during a summer college break.

He and Sandra were married in the house at Cama Beach after he finished law school.

He has been a lawyer in the U.S. Navy, a legal counsel for the Washington State House of Representatives, Executive Director of the Washington Environmental Council, an attorney in private practice, and a writer and sometime artist. He and Sandra live in a house he designed in a forested setting outside Olympia, Washington.

He considers his role helping Cama Beach become a state park, many details of which are included the book, to be some of the most important work of his life.

His other books include the award winning epic historical novels, *India Treasures* and *India Fortunes*.

He encourages your comments about this book. You may reach him by email at Gary@GaryWorthington.com.